COR HANDBOOI

COR FOLDER

FORMS

Printed by: 4th Watch Publishing Co. https://usgovpub.com

FORWARD

The Contracting Officer's Representative (COR) also known as the Contracting Officer's Technical Representative (COTR), has become an increasingly important person in the accomplishment of our assigned mission. We can write the best of contracts, and fail unless we have competent and dedicated CORs to monitor them, and to serve as communication links for assigned functions between the contractor and the Contracting Officer.

This handbook was designed to assist you with your assignment as a COR by identifying and explaining the many responsibilities normally associated with a COR. However, this handbook is not a regulation and is not a substitute for specific directions that are given to the COR by a Contracting Officer.

There is also a standardized ASC COR File that must be maintained by all ASC CORs. It is critical that all required information is maintained in the COR Folder and that records are up to date. ASC COR Files will be audited for compliance to the COR Folder requirements described in this handbook.

If you have any questions about your responsibilities and limitations, or any of the information contained in this handbook, contact your Contracting Officer for guidance.

ARMY SUSTAINMENT COMMAND

CONTRACTING OFFICER'S REPRESENTATIVE HANDBOOK

Table of Contents

SECTION I: COR SELECTION, DESIGNATION, QUALIFICATIONS, TRAINING, REVOCATION/TERMINATION

Selection

A Contracting Officer may select and designate, in writing, a qualified U.S. Government employee to act as a COR in administering a contract. Contractor personnel can not be appointed as CORs. The Contracting Officer may select only an individual who has qualifications and experience commensurate with the responsibilities to be assigned. The Supervisor or higher authority of the requiring activity, who is familiar with the requirement and the nominee's experience, training, and ability, will normally nominate the COR using Attachment 1 – Format for Nomination of Contracting Officer's Representative. The COR nominee may be one of the individuals who participated in developing the contract specification or work statement.

Designation

The Contracting Officer will set forth the CORs duties and limitations of authority in an appointment letter. The COR is authorized, within those limits, to ensure timely progress of contract performance and to provide effective technical guidance and advice to the Contracting Officer. A COR acting outside the limits of his authority may be held personally liable if a contractor incurs expense through unauthorized commitments. While a COR may act for the Contracting Officer in technical phases of the contract, he may not commit the government in matters which would change contract price, quantity, delivery schedule or other requirements of the contract. NOTE: All COR appointment letters shall use the format set forth in Attachment 2.

Qualifications

The Contracting Officer has sole authority for appointment of CORs and must by regulation; determine that the proposed COR has both the necessary technical and administrative competence and required training to perform COR duties in an effective and responsible manner. Accordingly, the nominating supervisor or higher authority, when requesting appointment of a COR, must certify the nomination of the COR in the format shown at Attachment 1 to ensure the COR nominee's compliance with DoDD 5500.7-R, The Joint Ethics Regulation (JER), and FAR 3.104, Procurement Integrity and to ensure the COR nominee's qualifications, to include:

    a. Knowledge of Government contracting processes.

    b. Familiarity with pertinent contract clauses such as Changes, Inspection and Acceptance, Government-Furnished Property, Termination, and the concepts of excusable and non-excusable delays in contract performance.

    c. Ability to document, analyze, interpret, and evaluate factors involved in contract administration.

    d. Previous on-the-job training or experience as COR (if applicable).

    e. Any formal education that may demonstrate necessary business acumen.

f. A listing of <u>all</u> contracts under which the COR nominee is currently performing COR duties and the name and phone number of the contracting officer.

g. Compliance with DoD 5500.7-R, the Joint Ethics Regulation (JER), and FAR 3.104, Procurement Integrity.

h. The certification for nomination of the COR and the record of the COR's qualifications will be maintained, with copies of the letters of appointment, in the applicable contract file. Each request for COR appointment must be accomplished by the certification and statement of qualifications detailed above (see Attachment 1 of the COR Handbook).

i. The COR nominee <u>must have the requisite security clearance</u> and sufficient time available to perform the COR duties. The nominee must give the Contracting Officer evidence that an <u>OGE Form 450 Confidential Financial Disclosure Report</u> has been officially filed. The nominees Supervisor should include a statement that the nominee has filed an OGE Form 450 in the nomination letter. Consideration should be given to the number of contracts currently being managed by the nominee when making this determination.

Training

COR Basic Training – The ASC requires that all CORs complete formal COR training before being appointed. The COR courses will be coordinated by the ASC G3 Training and Programs Division.   COR courses can be requested through the Total Employee Development (TED) System by searching on COR.

A 40 hour COR course is presented periodically during the year at ASC and other locations by the U.S. Army Logistics Management College (ALMC) and by contractors in every state. Contractor taught COR courses are offered by a variety of contractors. Contractor taught COR courses must be "equivalent" to the ALMC 40 hour course before they will be accepted by ASC. The Navy, Air Force, Defense Acquisition University, the Department of Defense and other government organizations also offer "equivalent" COR courses that may be accepted by ASC. If you are unsure verify the training with the ASC G3 Training and Programs Division to ensure the course will be accepted by ASC.

COR Refresher Training - DAU offers an 8 hour "COR With A Mission Focus" course which is available online at www.dau.mil. CORs should review the 40 hour course material frequently, but no less than annually. All COR's must complete this 8 hour online course every two years and certify they have completed the course. Plus they are to complete the Basic COR course every 3 years and provide the certification to ASC G3 Training.

Note: No one will be appointed as a COR based on taking only the COR Refresher Training online. DAU offers a 4 hour COR Overview Course online as well as the 8 hour COR With A Mission Focus course online but these do not satisfy the ASC COR Initial or 3 year training requirement.

Revocation/Termination of Appointment

The Contracting Officer may <u>revoke</u> the CORs appointment at any time. (Sample format at Attachment 3 of the COR Handbook.) Whenever a contract is completed, or a COR requests revocation of COR status due to transfer, retirement or other causes, the Contracting Officer must immediately revoke the CORs appointment. The Contracting Officer must sign the Revocation Letter and have the COR sign the Revocation Letter. If a COR requests relief from duties from the Contracting Officer, he must do so sufficiently in advance of reassignment or separation from the Government to permit the Contracting Officer to have adequate time to select, train and designate a successor, in writing (sample format at Attachment 3). CORs cannot re-delegate their authorities. CORs must return the signed copy of their appointment letter to the Contracting Officer <u>within 3 working days of receipt or the COR designation will be revoked</u>.

SECTION II: GENERAL COR DUTIES

The actions or inactions of a COR can convert a properly executed contract into an improper personal services one. The COR actions or inactions can also subject the Government to disputes, claims, and in some cases, can result in the COR being **personally liable** for his/her actions.

Individuals designated by the Contracting Officer as CORs are assigned specific responsibilities as set forth in their letters of appointment. Observe carefully the scope and limitations of the delegated authorities. If there are any doubts as to the correct course of action to be taken, contact the Contracting Officer. Specific responsibilities vary, but may include the following:

    a. Ensure full and complete coordination, cooperation and communication among Contractor, Contracting Officer and all Government personnel appropriately assigned to monitor contract performance to anticipate and resolve difficulties, and ensure satisfactory completion of contract.

    b. Carefully read and understand the terms and conditions of the contract (Including all modifications) and direct any questions as to content or interpretation to the Contracting Officer.

    c. Have ready access to all technical publications and regulations referenced in the contract.

    d. With the consent of the Contracting Officer, attend the post award conference so that all parties have a clear understanding of the scope of the contract, the technical requirements, and the rights and obligations of the parties.

    e. Perform periodic inspections and carefully monitor and keep the Contracting Officer informed of contractor performance of the technical requirements of the contract. Assure timely progress of the performance of the contract and that performance is within the scope of the work. In no event will the COR permit the Contractor to furnish materials or services in addition to, less than, or different from those required by the contract.

f. Exercise extreme caution in executing receipt and acceptance documents because, when performing this function, the COR is responsible for ensuring that the Government is receiving the end item or services for which it is paying.

g. Confirm or initiate all significant technical instructions to the contractor in writing, and provide a copy to the Contracting Officer.

h. Assure that changes in the work, services and resulting effects on delivery schedule are formally made by written supplemental agreement or change order issued by the Contracting Officer before the contractor proceeds with the changes.

i. Assure prompt review of draft reports and provide approval/disapproval/ comments to the contractor through the Contracting Officer.

j. Assure prompt inspection and acceptance, or rejection of services and/or deliverable items.

k. Refer to the Contracting Officer those matters, other than purely technical problems, which may affect the contract.

l. Furnish to the Contracting Officer a copy of the Government/contractor conference reports, trip reports, telephone conversation records, memorandum for record, and correspondence.

m. Sign all reports, trip reports, memorandum for record, appropriate correspondence, and all other related documents using your name, and title, followed by "Contracting Officer's Representative."

n. Coordinate with the Contracting Officer and with the Legal Office on the content of any contractually significant correspondence addressed to the contractor, in order to prevent possible misunderstandings or the creation of a condition that may be the basis of a later claim.

o. When appropriate, request the Contracting Officer authorize Government-Furnished Property, and when requested by the Contracting Officer, furnish disposition advice on Government-Furnished Property or contractor-acquired property.

p. Monitor financial management controls; coordinate with the Contracting Officer on all actions relating to funding and changes in the contract.

q. Furnish the Contracting Officer a notice of satisfactory or unsatisfactory completion of delivery or performance of a contract, purchase order, delivery order, or any modification thereto.

r. Report promptly and directly to the Contracting Officer on any suspected procurement fraud, bribery, conflicts of interest, or other improper conduct on the part of the contractor, its employees or other Government Officials.

s. For contracts that deal with classified information, security clearances have to be attained prior to contact award. Assure that the contractor maintains a current facility security clearance as well as clearance for personnel actually engaged in contract work, as it is determined that access to classified information will be required. It should be noted that there are absolutely no exceptions authorized for the release of classified information to contractors who do not possess a security clearance.

t. Provide recommendations to the Contracting Officer relative to approval/disapproval requests for public release of information regarding work being performed under the contract.

u. Notify the Contracting Officer of inventions by the contractor during the performance of the contract and assist the Contracting Officer in protecting the Government's interest.

v. When a final technical report is required by a CDRL on DD Form 1423 of the contract, upon acceptance of the contractor's final technical report, the COR shall prepare a memorandum for the PCOs signature, addressed to the contractor, Subject: Notice of Acceptance of Final Technical Report. Upon receipt of the PCOs signature, the COR shall forward the original memorandum to the contractor with additional copies as follows:

1 - Administrative Contracting Officer
1 - PCOs official contract file
1 - COR contract work file

w. Through surveillance of technical performance, assure that inefficient or wasteful methods are not being used.

x. Evaluate contractor requests for travel, to determine necessity of travel and reasonableness of costs.

y. Obtain Contracting Officer's approval for COR or other Government personnel travel to the contractor's facilities, and within seven (7) days after return, furnish the Contracting Officer with a trip report.

z. Review the contractor's invoice to insure that labor hours and materials charged to the contract are accurate. This can be done by checking time cards, in/out signing cards, and for materials, by obtaining copies of invoices. The contractor's invoices should accurately reflect the work completed and that the materials purchased are within the requirements of the contract.

aa. Furnish a monthly report to the Contracting Officer as to contract performance (Sample format at Attachment 4). If other than monthly reports (daily, weekly etc.) are required, the PCO will tailor to contract requirements and include in the Letter of Appointment.

ab. Inform the Contracting Officer when a contractor is known to be behind schedule, with the reasons therefore, and coordinate with the Contracting Officer corrective actions necessary to restore the contract schedule.

ac. Evaluate monthly cost and performance data on a quantitative and qualitative basis to include trends and projections.

ad. Surface any restriction on technical data to the Contracting Officer and Legal Office before acceptance.

ae. Maintain and keep current the COR contract work file (see Section IV).

af. Furnish the Contracting Officer with a formal request for termination of your COR appointment, when it is required (Sample format at Attachment 3).

ag. Constructive Changes - The COR shall not give any director or guidance to contractors, either orally or in writing, which might be interpreted as a change in the scope or terms of the contract. The COR is responsible only for giving technical guidance to assure that the technical scope and terms of the contract are met. An informal request for additional work caused by some act, or omission to act on the part of the Government which causes a contractor extra work, delay or expense is known as a constructive change and must be avoided. These types of changes sometimes lead to disputes and claims. **AFARS 5153.9001 Para 3 states that CORs may be held personally liable for unauthorized acts.**

ah. Preparation of Correspondence - The COR must sign all correspondence, reports, findings, recommendations, and other documents using his/her name followed by "Contracting Officer's Representative." The COR should communicate with the contractor, Contracting Officer, disbursing officer and others directly concerned with contract performance. All correspondence must reference the contract number.

ai. Correspondence with Contractors - The COR must forward to the Contracting Officer a copy of any correspondence to the contractor with appropriate explanation if not apparent from the text. The COR must also forward to the Contracting Officer the original of the correspondence received from the contractor and coordinate with the Contracting Officer and the Legal Office on the content of any contractually significant correspondence addressed to the contractor, in order to prevent possible misunderstandings or the creation of a condition that may be the basis of a later claim. The Contracting Officer will advise the COR of the appropriate mail system to be used (e.g., certified mail, etc.).

aj. DD Form 250, Invoices or Vouchers or Wide Area Work Flow - The COR will promptly sign all DD Form 250's, invoices or vouchers after verifying receipt of a deliverable. The COR will immediately forward copies to the Contracting Officer, the payment office and make any other distribution.

NOTE:

The above are only general COR duties. If you are being appointed as COR for a Personal Services contract there will be additional guidance provided. See your specific Letter of Appointment, and the Quality Assurance Surveillance Plan if there is one for your contract, for duties and limitations applicable to your specific contract. Such duties and limitations may be different for different contracts if you are a COR for more than one contract. **KNOW THE REQUIREMENTS WITHIN YOUR COR APPOINTMENT LETTER. KNOW ALL THE TERMS AND PROVISIONS OF THE SPECIFIC CONTRACT.**

SECTION III: APPOINTMENT OF CONTRACTING OFFICER'S REPRESENTATIVE

Detailed policies, authorities, limitations, responsibilities and COR qualifications are provided in DFARS 201.602-2 and AFARS 5153.9001.

The Procuring Contracting Officer (PCO) may select and appoint a COR, as required, to assist with various contract administration tasks. In accordance with DFARS 201.602-70, insert clause DFARS 252.201-7000 Contracting Officer's Representative in solicitations and contracts when appointment of a COR is anticipated. Although the request for COR nomination is initiated by the requesting activity by submitting a written request for COR nomination to the PCO (Attachment 1), appointment of a COR is the Contracting Officer's decision/function. The Contracting Officer will specifically designate the CORs responsibilities and limitations of authority in the COR Letter of Appointment in accordance with the format beginning at Attachment 2. The COR is authorized within the designated limits to ensure timely progress of contract performance and to provide effective technical guidance to the Contracting Officer.

In selecting an individual for designation as an authorized representative, the Contracting Officer shall ensure that the individual possesses qualifications and experience commensurate with the authority with which he/she is to be empowered. To ensure this, the requiring activity shall submit to the Contracting Officer a nomination resume of the proposed CORs experience, qualifications, and training, certified by the nominating COR's supervisor or higher authority (Attachment 1).

Personnel appointed by the Contracting Officer to assist in contract administration shall be identified as a Contracting Officer Representative (COR). No other title is authorized by ASC.

The Contracting Officer will ensure that CORs have been personally and clearly briefed on the functions to be performed and the limitations of authority being delegated. The appointees will then sign the Letter of Appointment, which will be placed in the contract file. A copy will be given to the appointees to be placed in the COR file. If the COR does not receive this briefing or has not signed the COR Letter of Appointment, the COR must see the Contracting Officer <u>before</u> performing COR duties or communicating with the contractor.

The Contracting Officer will furnish a copy of the letter appointing the COR to the Contractor. Acknowledgment of receipt of the letter must be made by the contractor.

The COR is not authorized to change any of the terms and conditions of the contract. Changes, including changes in the Statement of Work, will be made only by the Contracting Officer by properly executed modifications to the contract. A COR acting outside the limits of his/her authority does so at his/her own peril. He/She may be held personally liable for unauthorized acts if a Contractor incurs expense through unauthorized commitments. (AFARS 5153.9001 Para 3).

SECTION IV: COR FILES

Establishment

The COR must establish and maintain a current, separate file for each contract being administered. This file must be available for review by the Contracting Officer, Inspector General, Government Accountability Office, Army Audit Agency, Internal Review, or any other official government authorized by the Contracting Officer. The COR Files must be maintained in accordance with the standardized ASC COR File format.

The COR should also have a copy of this handbook for guidance. The COR Handbook is revised on a regular basis and it is available online for download at the ASC homepage or review at the ASC G3 Training Knowledge Center AKO websites.

Content

As a minimum, the file must contain:

      a. A copy of the signed, dated and acknowledged COR appointment letter.

      b. A copy of the contract and all modifications and/or delivery orders thereto.

      c. Memorandums for the record or minutes of pre-performance conferences.

      d. All correspondence between COR and the contractor, Contracting Officer, or others concerning performance of the contract; together with English translations of all correspondence written in a foreign language.

      e. Memorandum of all telephone conversations which relate in any way to the contract.

      f. A copy of the trip report of every visit that has been made to the contractor's facility. A copy of this report must be provided to the Contracting Officer within seven (7) days after each visit. The trip report must contain persons contacted, dates, items discussed and actions taken.

      g. A copy of the minutes of all meetings and conferences with the contractor. These minutes should include persons present, dates, matters discussed and actions taken.

h. A copy of all approvals the COR has given to the contractor. These approvals can only be within the COR-designated authority.

i. Copies of progress schedules of work approved by the Contracting Officer, if applicable, and schedule of cumulative payments approved.

j. Copies of all data, reports and other documentation furnished by the contractor; the COR's analysis of it, action taken and the date of such action.

k. Records of any inspections performed under the contract including when and how the inspections were accomplished and the results.

l. Copies of all surveillance plans and a record of each individual surveillance conducted, the results thereof, and any actions taken.

m. Copies of all DD Form 250's, invoices, vouchers and receipt documents processed, including COR recommendations relating to them.

n. Any other documentation and data necessary to provide a complete history of all actions taken under, or in connection with the contract by the COR.

o. A copy of the COR Training Certificate or a current valid Contracting Officer Warrant or a Waiver of COR Training Based Upon Experience For CORs Appointed Prior To 11/01/2005 signed by the Principal Assistant Responsible For Contracting (PARC).

NOTE: As a minimum, all documents must be signed and dated by the COR. Other signatures may be required, depending on the nature of the document.

Maintenance

The COR file must be maintained as follows:

a. A copy of each appointment letter and the basic contract with all modifications and/or delivery orders thereto.

b. All other documents in chronological sequence. It is recommended that the types of document be identified accordingly; memoranda for record, inspections, trip reports, minutes of meetings, emails, conferences, etc., for rapid access by the COR and/or inspection by authorized officials.

c. Annually, the COR will schedule an appointment with the Contracting Officer for review of the COR file.

Disposition of COR Files

Upon termination of a COR appointment, the COR must promptly transfer the COR files to the successor COR, or forward them to the Contracting Officer, whichever is instructed by the Contracting Officer. Upon completion of the contract, the COR must forward the COR files to the Contracting Officer for inclusion in the official contract file.

SECTION V: ACTIONS TO BE TAKEN WHEN A COR EXCEEDS HIS/HER AUTHORITY

For the first instance of improper action, the Contracting Officer will prepare a letter to the COR pointing out the improper action and reminding the COR of the limitations of his/her authority under his/her COR appointment. It will specifically reserve the right of the Government to take further action against the individual for his/her improper acts. The letter will be forwarded to the COR through his/her activity head (Director, Commander, etc.). It will be signed by the Contracting Officer and will contain a warning that if there are further instances of improper actions, the offender's COR appointment may be terminated.

For the second offense by the same COR (whether or not on the same or another contract), the individual's COR appointment may be revoked for all contracts for which the individual has been named COR. Prior to taking the action, the Contracting Officer will coordinate, through the ASC chain of command to the appropriate Director of Contracting (DOC) and Commander.

In cases of gross abuse, the Contracting Officer will revoke the COR appointment immediately without giving the COR a second chance (Sample format at Attachment 5). A copy will be included in the contract file. An additional copy will be forwarded, for information, to the ASC. Additionally, the contracting officer will take any other actions required by law or regulation such as, when appropriate, referring the action to the Contract Adjustment Board (PL 85-804), after taking other actions required by ACA/DA.

If a COR exceeds his/her authority, the procedures for ratification of an unauthorized commitment are set forth in FAR 1.602-3. Cases that are not ratifiable under FAR 1.602-3 may be subject to resolution as authorized by FAR Part 50. Such procedures often require high level approval (outside the ACC, Rock Island Contracting Center) and are discretionary in nature by the approving official. In the event the approval official does not elect to use his/her discretion to reimburse the contractor for acts exceeding the CORs authority, the COR may be held personally liable for any costs or damages incurred by the contractor or the Government.

SECTION VI: SURVEILLANCE PLANS

Objective

Not every contract, delivery order or task order requires a surveillance plan, which with performance work statements is the Quality Assurance Surveillance Plan. A surveillance plan is mandatory for Time and Material contracts. The following is offered when a surveillance plan is needed:

The objective of contract surveillance is to monitor contractor performance to assure the services received are (1) timely, and (2) consistent with contract quality requirements. To be effective, contract surveillance requires appropriate and immediate on-site monitoring of the services being performed. On-site monitoring should include periodic verification and analysis of the services performed. The effectiveness of contract surveillance depends on keeping the Contracting Officer timely informed of deviations from the contractual requirements. (OFPP Pamphlet 4, Chapter 4, The Surveillance Plan). The objective of surveillance is to determine if and when to intercede take corrective action and when required terminate a contract, and if and when to exercise contractual options.

Surveillance plans should contain the sampling guides and activity checklists to monitor required services essential to contractor performance. The plan's objective should be to ensure adequate and timely performance of the service rather than how the services are accomplished.

The surveillance plan is attached by the Contracting Officer to the COR appointment letter and made a part thereof; or incorporated in full text in the responsibilities and limitations of the appointment letter. Whatever way the Contracting Officer determines the method of inclusion, the surveillance procedures shall be discussed at a post-award conference, or otherwise with all parties concerned to assure uniform understanding and the file documented accordingly (FAR 42.5).

Note: The Surveillance Plan is shared with the contractor and the DCMA.

Composition and Method

The plan should be developed by the initiating/requiring activity in conjunction with the statement of work, and tailored to meet specific contract requirements and operating conditions.

As a minimum, the following elements and method of accomplishment are suggested to be incorporated in the surveillance plan:

   a. Provide a schedule for periodic on-site inspections, floor checks, and audits of contractor's billings to ensure costs being charged to the contract are legitimate and reasonable.

   METHOD - Set forth the frequency (once a week, monthly, etc) an inspection will be made.

b. Set forth what will be checked during an inspection, how it will be checked, and whether random samples or 100% inspection will be performed.

METHOD - Once every month an inspection of technical bulletin revisions will be made to determine quality of work and progress toward completion. The revisions will be read for quality and accuracy. Random sampling will be done as work progresses. Near contract completion a 100% inspection will be done.

c. Describe the method that will be used for checking cost type contract invoices to assure that only those labor categories used for the performance of a task or project are invoiced to the Government. Describe how material or products will be delivered and accepted under a cost or fixed price type contract.

METHOD - Set forth the frequency that time cards and payroll records will be inspected. Set forth a specific policy for delivery and acceptance procedures.

d. Determine how you will assure the Contracting Officer that the prime contractor has obtained adequate competition when acquiring materials for cost type contracts.

METHOD - State in the surveillance plan that contractor's acquisition of materials by competition will be checked for charges over a reasonable amount of money (state amount you feel will be reasonable).

e. Determine how you will assure that progress payments do not exceed the quality and quantity of work completed and payment is made in accordance with the progress payment clause.

METHOD - State that before approval for a progress payment is given by the Contracting Officer you will make an inspection to determine if the quantity and quality of work is in accordance with the contract requirements, and the work completed to date justifies the amount of payment to be made.

Increased surveillance should be made when the Contractor begins to experience problems or difficulties in performance, financial strength, management, quality assurance, or its accounting system. Because the surveillance plan is a tool to be used by the Government, it can be modified at any time it is determined to be necessary. Keeping the Contracting Officer informed is mandatory for the successful completion of a contract.

In monitoring the contractor or in-house work force's performance, various inspection methods can be used. The following is a brief description of the most common and the considerations for their use:

a. Random sampling - This is the preferred surveillance method because it provides a non-biased, comprehensive evaluation of the contractor's performance with an efficient utilization of limited inspector personnel. The Government inspection personnel need only make relatively few observations from which they can project the quality of the entire lot. The contractor does not know which service output will be observed; consequently, all must be done correctly, and the Government Inspector is prevented from biasing the sample by his own judgment. The advantage is that the results can be projected to the lot, without inspecting the entire lot.

b. Planned sampling - This type of sampling is normally used to check the contractor's quality control system to ensure the contractor's inspection system is capable of meeting the Government's quality requirements. Because defects found as the result of planned sampling cannot be considered statistically valid for purposes of evaluating the entire work lot, monetary deductions for other than satisfactory performance are limited to only the work specifically found defective. For this reason, planned sampling should not be used as the only method of surveillance. When planned sampling is used, work process outputs are selected in accordance with subjective criteria established in the surveillance plan. These criteria should be documented and applied consistently throughout the observation period and from one period to the next. Surveillance consistency enables the inspector to detect trends in performance and requires less inspector retraining time and document/report revisions. The advantages to this method are that Government inspectors can focus their attention on known problem areas and the contractor or in-house work force has a greater incentive to improve those deficient areas that they know will be observed. The disadvantage is that because the observations are not selected randomly, comparisons of quality cannot be made between the sampled outputs and the lot.

c. 100 percent inspection - As the name implies, all outputs in the designated lot would be observed by the Inspector. For example, with a service requirement for required reports, all reports listed in the lot would be examined for acceptance.

d. Customer complaints. Outputs observed are not selected by the inspector, but are based on written or telephonic complaints made by customers. Once received, the Inspector will investigate the complaint and, if validated, it will be annotated as a deficiency against the contractor.

Each inspection made by Government inspectors must be scheduled, documented, and filed for further reference, audit, and proof of inspection. Other interactions between Government inspectors and the contractor (for example, customer complaints, unsatisfactory contract performance, equipment breakdown, and meetings) should also be documented and filed. This documentation could be in the form of a contract deficiency report, minutes of meetings, annotations on tally checklists, correspondence, and so forth.

Further guidance on these surveillance tools is set forth In Office of Federal Procurement Policy (OFPP) Pamphlet 4, Chapter 4, The Surveillance Plan. See Attachment 6 for a sample Time and Material Contract Surveillance Plan.

SECTION VII: COR DUTIES - TASK ORDER CONTRACTS

Introduction

Task order contracts are used to support, not directly perform, an organization's mission, and are normally available for use by the entire customer organization, rather than a segment thereof. These contracts permit relatively quick response to performance of tasks for which no in-house capability exists, or of an effort that is temporarily beyond the workload capacity of an organization's employees. Because of the very nature of such contracts, however, they provide the opportunity for abuse and/or abrogation of the traditional checks and balances in DOD Acquisition. For this reason, it is desirable for each contracting activity within ASC to have policies and procedures established toward assuring that control of task order contracts remains within the contracting activity. No regulation or procedure, however, can be substituted for the common sense, diligence, and the firm and proper application of authority by the Contracting Officer.

Task order contracts must be managed in a manner to prevent the appearance of personal services, (employee-employer relationship between Government and contractor employees), co-mingling or co-locating Government and contractor employees in ways which induce personal service relationships, and organizational conflicts of interest. The intent is that the Government does not tell the contractor to make Government decisions, and that the Government does not require or allow the contractor to perform tasks inherently Governmental in nature.

Only the Contracting Officer is authorized to issue task orders that obligate monies. The COR is responsible to the Contracting Officer and is limited to the responsibilities and authorities set forth in the appointment letter.

The COR shall maintain a written workload plan to be utilized in task order management and control under the contract. This plan shall be placed in a separate folder, identified, and made a part of the COR file.

Instructions to Contractors

Prior to commencement of performance, the Contracting Officer/COR must ensure that the contractor is instructed as to:

    a. Authority, responsibilities and limitations of the COR.

    b. Clear understanding of the contract terms and conditions.

    c. Applicable security requirements.

    d. Clear understanding of inspection, acceptance, and invoicing procedures.

The above can be accomplished by the Contracting Officer arranging a post-award conference, or otherwise, with all interested parties.

Monthly Reports

On an established date of each month, or sooner if determined by the Contracting Officer, the COR must certify, in writing, that to the best of the CORs knowledge and belief:

 a. That a review of the tasks assigned indicates no instances of personal services.

 b. That a review of the tasks assigned indicates no instances where work requested/performed is beyond the scope of the contract.

 c. That the contractor is, or is not, performing within cost or schedule of the task order. In cases where the contractor is not performing within cost or delivery schedule, the COR will identify the specific nature of the problem and recommend remedial action to the Contracting Officer. However, the Contracting Officer will make the final determination as to what action to take.

This certification will be added to the COR report (Sample format at Attachment 4). Also see Section III, General COR duties, Paragraph aa.

Surveillance Plan

A surveillance plan (Sample format at Attachment 6) for monitoring the contractor's performance shall be prepared (mandatory for time-and-material contracts (FAR 16.601)) and submitted as a part of the Acquisition Requirements Package (ARP). It is recommended that the surveillance plan be written at the time the statement of work is written and be tailored accordingly. It should include, but not be limited to, the following:

 a. The number and frequency of on-site floor checks/inspections that will be made during the contract term.

 b. A method for tracking labor hours and materials used on a specific contract for repairs made at the location. This can be done by setting up in/out signing sheets as the contractor arrives and leaves the location.

 Example:

 1. Contract number/Task Order number
 2. Item description/model number;
 3. Date/time of arrival and departure;
 4. Contract titles of labor categories of individuals assigned to do repairs;
 5. Time spent effecting repair;
 6. Description of malfunction and action taken;
 7. Part(s) replaced;
 8. Non-problem maintenance performed (cleaning, etc.);
 9. Signature of service technician;
 10. Signature of COR.

Processing Contractor's Invoices:

The COR can obtain copies of invoices from the contractor for purchases of materials.

     c. A procedure for checking the accuracy of labor hours and materials used for work performed other than at ASC, as they are invoiced. This can be done by checking time cards and assuring the labor hours were used for the instant contract. Again, the materials can be checked by obtaining copies of the contractor's purchase invoices.

     d. A method to assure that inefficient or wasteful methods are not being used by the contractor. One way this can being done is by determining if the contractor is using competitive methods for acquiring materials.

     e. A method for keeping track of the funding expended under task orders versus the ceiling amount of the contract, and the balance remaining to be placed under contract. Record of the 5 percent withholding by the Contracting Officer of the labor rates total from each invoice shall be incorporated in the tracking. Periodically, the balance remaining shall be compared with the balance record being maintained by the Contracting Officer.

     f. If there is a disagreement over the items or other information, the Contracting Officer's designated representative shall note exceptions thereon, so that the matter may be resolved by the Contracting Officer under the terms of the contract. For acceptance of services other than those performed under a Cost Reimbursement, Time and Materials, or a Labor Hour Contract, a DD Form 250 Material Inspection and Receiving Report is utilized. The Contracting Officer will provide the COR the specific duties they will have for processing payments, DD Form 250's or other documentation.

     g. Effective 1 October 1999, all payments processed by the DFAS Accounts Payable and Vendor Pay Office, will be made by Electronic Funds Transfer (EFT). Contracting Officers and CORs, if required, are reminded to register all contracts in the Central Contractor Register (CCR) database. The CCR registration web site is http://ccr.edi.disa.mil . The vendor's tax identification number is also required on all payments. All paying offices will return contracts or invoices without payment effective 1 October 1999 when EFT information is missing. Return the documents to paying office no later than 7 days after receipt, which will stop the EDA clock and avoid interest penalties. Ensure the request for EFT information accompanies the returned contract or invoice. The only EFT waivers/exemptions permitted are: (a.) sole proprietorship. This category is input by the vendor when registering in the CCR, (b.) non-recurring payments also referred to as one-time payments as identified in the contract, (c.) all government agencies, federal, state and local, (d.) all foreign vendors, (e.) classified vouchers, (f.) government bills of lading, and (g.) utilities.

The above are a few of the specific responsibilities that shall be considered for surveillance of task order contracts. Refer to "General COR Duties" for additional responsibilities that may be applicable, and also incorporate those responsibilities that are tailored to the contract that will require surveillance.

Payment Procedures:

COR shall follow any payment procedures set forth in the COR Appointment Letter. The Prompt Payment Act of 1982 and other laws require the Government to pay interest when specified lead times are exceeded. This reduces ASC funds available for other purposes. Therefore, IT IS EMPHASIZED that expediting payment to contractors is mandatory so that payments can be made within the time constraints required by regulation. Interest payments shall be avoided. See Attachment No. 11, DFAS Vendor Pay Procedures.

SECTION VIII: COR DUTIES - SERVICE CONTRACTS

Instructions to Contractors:

Prior to commencement, the PCO must ensure that the contractor is instructed as to:

    a. Authority, responsibilities and limitations of the COR.

    b. Clear understanding of the contract terms and conditions.

    c. Applicable security requirements.

    d. Applicable value engineering provisions.

    e. Clear understanding of inspection, acceptance, and invoicing procedures.

The above can be accomplished by the Contracting Officer/COR arranging a Post Award conference with all interested parties.

Contractor Inspection Records

The contractor is required by the contract clause, "Inspection of... depending on what type of contract (e.g. "Inspection of Services-Fixed-Price" (FAR 52.246-4)) to provide and maintain an inspection system acceptable to the Government covering the services to be performed under the contract. The "Inspection of Services-Fixed Price" clause further requires the contractor to keep complete records of contractor-performed inspections and to make such records available to the Government during the term of the contract. As a minimum, the contractor's records must indicate the nature of the observations, the number of observations made, and the number and type of deficiencies found. The inspection records must also indicate the acceptability of the services and actions taken to correct deficiencies. The COR must ensure that the contractor complies with this contract requirement.

COR Suspense System

The COR must establish a suspense system to advise the Contracting Officer of the contractor's failure to complete performance or delivery in accordance with the contract schedule. COR reporting of contractor failures should not wait for the monthly report.

Notifications to Contracting Officer

The COR must promptly inform the Contracting Officer of the following:

a. The exact date the contractor began performance.

b. Incidents of unsatisfactory performance by the contractor, specifying the applicable paragraph of the contract which has been violated by the contractor and the circumstances surrounding the violation with names, dates and places.

c. Delays in the contractor's progress due to the fault of the Government and a recommendation to the Contracting Officer regarding any extensions of the contract completion date.

d. Any discrepancy between actual conditions and those represented in the contract provisions, specifications or drawings.

Correction of Deficiencies

The contract clause entitled, "Inspection of ... (depending on the contract) specifies inspection rights of the Government and provides remedies if the contractor's work does not conform with the requirements of the contract. If the contractor services are not in conformity with the contract requirements, the COR may request the contractor to correct the deficiencies noted so that performance will comply with the requirements of the contract, at no additional increase in total contract amount. If these services are of such a nature that the defect cannot be corrected, the COR may advise the contractor to take necessary action to ensure that future performance of services conform with the requirements of the contract. In addition, the COR must promptly advise the Contracting Officer so that the contract price can be reduced to reflect the reduced value of the services performed. If the contractor fails to promptly perform the services again, or to take necessary action to ensure future performance of the services in conformity with the requirements of the contract, the Government, through the Contracting Officer, has the right either to:

a. Have the services performed by contract or otherwise in conformity with the contract requirements, charging the contractor any costs occasioned to the Government which are directly related to the performance of such services, or

b. Terminate the contract for default as provided in the contract clause entitled, "Default (Fixed-Price Supply and Service)" (FAR 52.249-8).

Contractual Rights of the Government

It may be in the best interest of the Government not to reject the non-conforming materials or services because of:

a. The urgency of the need for the services and the period of time required to obtain them from other sources, as compared with the time delivery could be obtained from the delinquent contractor;

b. The availability of the services from other sources;

c. Any other pertinent facts and circumstances.

If it is desired to accept work which essentially meets the needs of the Government but does not conform to the requirements of the contract, the COR must furnish the Contracting Officer recommendations to accept the work together with findings of all points in which the work fails to meet contract requirements and an estimate of the time required for the contractor to complete performance. The Contracting Officer may extend the contract completion date by formal modification to allow the contractor to correct deficient work.

Preparation of Correspondence

The COR must sign all correspondence, reports, findings, recommendations, and other documents using name and title, followed by "Contracting Officer's Representative." The COR should communicate with the contractor, Contracting Officer, disbursing officer and others directly concerned with contract performance. All correspondence must reference the contract number.

Correspondence with Contractors

The COR must forward to the Contracting Officer a copy of any correspondence to the contractor with appropriate explanation if not apparent from the text. The COR must also forward to the Contracting Officer the original of the correspondence received from the contractor. Coordinate with the Contracting Officer on the content of any contractually significant correspondence addressed to the contractor, in order to prevent possible misunderstandings or the creation of a condition that may be the basis of a later claim. The Contracting Officer will advise the COR of the appropriate mail system to be used (e.g., certified mail).

Payment Procedure

In accordance with the contract clause entitled, "Payments" (FAR 52.232-1), the contractor is entitled to payments for services rendered and accepted. The COR Appointment letter sets forth the CORs responsibilities regarding payment procedures.

The Prompt Payment Act of 1982 and other laws require the Government to pay interest when specified lead times are exceeded. This reduces ASC funds available for other purposes. Therefore, IT IS EMPHASIZED that expediting payment to the contractors is mandatory so that payment can be made within the time constraints required by regulation. Interest payments shall be avoided. See Attachment 11, DFAS Vendor Pay Procedures.

Value Engineering Change Proposals (VECP)

The COR should encourage the contractor to submit VE Change Proposals to the Contracting Officer for processing. These proposals are provided by the contractor if they see processes that can improve performance and cost.

SECTION IX: INFORMATION TECHNOLOGY

Introduction

     a. Contracting for IT resources is accomplished by following the procedures set forth in Federal Acquisition Regulation (FAR) Part 39, Acquisition of Information Technology, Defense Federal Acquisition Regulation Supplement (DFARS) Part 239, and Army Federal Acquisition Regulation Supplement (AFARS) Part 5139, and AR 25-1, Army Information Management. AR 25-1 has been re-written and is currently in DA LEGAL for final review before implementation. The new AR 25-1 implements PL 104-106, Division E of the Clinger-Cohen Act of 1996 plus other public laws and directives.

     b. The new AR 25-1 will require each MACOM Commander to develop and maintain internal headquarters and MACOM-wide Information Management/ Information Technology (IM/IT) procedures to provide required guidance and direction to subordinate organizations. Until the new AR 25-1 is implemented, the current AR 25-1 and AMC PAM 25-34 remain in effect. They specify that prior to Information Technology (IT) resources being acquired by ASC activities, validation and certification of requirements must be in place prior to solicitation.

Acquisition of Commercial Items

Other parts of the FAR, such as FAR Part 12, may apply when the IT being purchased is a commercial item.

Instructions to Contractors

Prior to commencement of performance, the Contracting Officer/COR must ensure that the contractor is instructed as to:

    a. Authority, responsibilities and limitations of the COR.

    b. Clear understanding of the contract terms and conditions.

    c. Clear understanding of inspection, acceptance, and invoicing procedures.

The above can be accomplished by the Contracting Officer/COR arranging a pre-performance conference, or otherwise with all interested parties.

Surveillance

It is the CORs responsibility to ensure that equipment delivered and maintenance for equipment fulfill the requirements of the contract. The COR surveillance shall include, but not be limited to, the following:

a. Assure site preparation is completed before delivery of equipment/system. Otherwise the contractor may invoice for storage charges if delivery cannot be made on the contract delivery date.

b. The COR shall advise the Contracting Officer, in writing, of the commencement date of the performance and acceptance of the equipment/system.

c. Relative to the above inspection process, prepare a tracking method in the event the equipment/system malfunctions, and the performance period has to start from the beginning or the equipment/system cannot meet the functional criteria. Before acceptance, the COR shall be assured that the equipment/system meets the requirements set forth in the contract.

d. Assure that equipment is immediately installed upon delivery and working, so that the commercial warranty is not violated.

e. Prepare a method for tracking labor hours and parts used for repairs made at ASC. This can be done by setting up in/out signing sheets as the contractor arrives and leaves ASC. Example:

   (1) Contract Number/Task number;
   (2) Item description/model number;
   (3) Date/time of arrival and departure;
   (4) Time spent effecting repair;
   (5) Description of malfunction and action taken;
   (6) Part(s) replaced;
   (7) Non-problem maintenance performed (cleaning, etc.);
   (8) Signature of service technician;
   (9) Signature of COR.

The COR can obtain copies of invoices from the contractor for purchases of parts.

f. A method to insure that inefficient or wasteful methods are not being used by the contractor to acquire parts. One way this can be done is by determining if the contractor is using competitive methods of acquisition.

g. When commercial software and/or software development are acquired, assure that the software functional requirements of the contract are met. Prepare a documentation method to use during inspection.

h. Assure that proprietary rights of software contractors are not violated. Any violation may involve litigation and incur costs to the Government.

The above are a few of the specific COR responsibilities for surveillance of contracts for IT resources. For additional guidance, refer to "General COR Duties" (see Section III) for other responsibilities that may be applicable, and those duties set forth in your COR Letter of Appointment. Many contracts for IT resources are of a time-and-material task order contract nature, so CORs should review Section VIII, for other applicable guidance.

SECTION X: DISPUTES AND APPEALS

Disputes between a contractor and the Contracting Officer may occur under a contract. It is important that differences with the contractor, which may arise, do not interfere with timely performance of the contract. All contracts contain a Disputes clause that presents the procedures to be followed in case of any unresolved disagreements between contractors and the Contracting Officer. The COR will play a key role in advising the Contracting Officer as to the intent of specifications or provisions of the contract that may be the subject of dispute. Therefore, the COR should know the contract and create and keep the necessary documentation required to state a position, in writing, to help the Contracting Officer. The Contracting Officer must respond promptly with a written decision, including the reasons for each dispute received. Unless appealed within certain time limits, the Contracting Officer's decision becomes final and is not subject to review. The COR should be aware that the Government has to pay interest on claims that might be in dispute. Therefore, it is imperative that the COR provide the Contracting Officer with the necessary documentation promptly.

The DFARS 233.2 and AFARS 5133.2 provide specific instructions concerning disputes, Contracting Officer decisions and appeals.

CORs should be prepared to be responsive to the need for them to submit various forms of documentation and correspondence developed during the course of an acquisition. Frequently, the occasion may arise to give verbal testimony before the Government Accountability Office (GAO), the General Services Administration Board of Contract Appeals (GSBCA), the Armed Services Board of Contract Appeals (ASBCA) or a court of the judicial system in connection with disputes or other contractual matters. The completeness, accuracy and currency of the CORs records may determine who prevails, the Government or the contractor.

SECTION XI: COR DO'S AND DON'TS

This section is designed to provide a quick reference listing, though not all inclusive, of general Do's and Don'ts for a COR. These should be covered by the Contracting Officer when the COR is given his COR letter.

    a. DO retain your appointment letter. This letter tells you the exact functions that have been delegated to you. Know its contents. Acknowledge its receipt and return the copy to the Contracting Officer.

    b. DO understand the limitations of your authority.

    c. DO have a complete copy of the contract and all modifications/delivery orders readily available.

    d. DO immediately familiarize yourself with all the terms and conditions of the contract.

    e. DO establish and maintain a file for all documents, conversations, and correspondence pertaining to the contract. This file is to be forwarded to the Contracting Officer for inclusion in the official file after completion of contract.

    f. DO give prompt attention to correspondence and other actions requiring your approval.

    g. DO spot check the contractor's work to see that it is completed in a timely and proper manner. Perform more intensive and fairly continuous surveillance on those contracts that require it.

    h. DO complete the required performance reports thoroughly and accurately to enable the Contracting Officer to properly evaluate the contractor.

    i. DO enforce correction of deficient work. Be cautious, however, as you are not authorized to personally supervise any contractor employee (See Attachment 10).

    j. DO assure that the contractor responds in a timely manner when required. Be sure all responses are accurate.

    k. DO report personnel deficiencies to the contractor's site supervisor and to the Contracting Officer.

    l. DO verify to the Contracting Officer the need for contractor overtime when requested by the contractor.

    m. DO report all actual overtime.

    n. DO assure satisfactory subcontractor performance by observing contractor's surveillance. Report inadequate surveillance to the Contracting Officer.

o. DO follow through on corrective actions recommended by any authorized inspector (or team of inspectors).

p. DO ascertain that all emergencies are attended to and resolved immediately. Coordinate fully with the Contracting Officer.

q. DO inform the contractor immediately when you become aware of any unsatisfactory performance. The Contracting Officer will assist you in obtaining corrective action. Differences of opinion between you and the contractor that cannot be resolved at your level should be referred to the Contracting Officer. Recommend to the contractor that he also refer the conflict to his superior. Make it clear to him that both of you must abide by the decisions made by the Contracting Officer. In doing this do not take any action that may be construed as an actual or constructive change.

r. DO report to the Contracting Officer any labor disputes or problems which have a potential for impairing the contractor's ability to perform.

s. DO put Instructions to the contractor in writing. Ensure that such instructions are within the scope of your authority. Failure to do so may create problems for you and your replacement, as well as to the Contracting Officer. Remember, only the Contracting Officer can award a delivery order for tasks on a task order contract.

t.   DO document all actions and decisions and date all documents.

u. DO document the date, time, place, and persons involved in all meetings with the contractor or his personnel.

v. DO ensure that your replacement is thoroughly briefed, both verbally and in writing, on all important issues.

w. DO be aware of your relationship with the contractor and avoid even the appearance of an unethical or illegal action.

x. DO use clear, accurate, performance-oriented language and express only the Government's actual minimum needs when writing the work statement.

y. DO protect contractor proprietary information when doing estimates or reports.

z. DO advise the Contracting Officer, at the time a procurement request is initiated, that the item is foreign made, if this fact is known.

aa.DO assure that any Government-financed training is not for the basics that should have been provided by the contractor.

ab. DO endorse "visit request" and "need-to-know" documents prior to Contracting Officer approval. This also includes verification of classification status (SECRET, etc.).

ac. DO discuss unusual problems/situations/urgent requirements with the Contracting Officer prior to taking any actions - something often can be worked out within the prescribed regulations.

ad. DO prepare truly Independent Government Cost Estimates. Don't get them from a prospective contractor.

ae. DO read DoD 5500.7-R, The Joint Ethics Regulation for Department of Defense Personnel, and its implementations.

af. DO familiarize yourself with the Procurement integrity Act (FAR 3.104).

ag. DO coordinate all engineering changes affecting a contract with all cognizant segments and agencies. Prior to discussing with the contractor, discuss it with the Contracting Officer. Changes may only be made through modifying the contract.

ah. DON'T split quantities in order to circumvent procedures/regulations and approvals required for higher dollar value procurements.

ai. DON'T take any action which will obligate, or give the appearance of obligating, the Government financially or otherwise. Only the Contracting Officer has this authority.

aj. DON'T solicit for "unsolicited proposals."

ak. DON'T contact contractors and give them information about upcoming procurements.

al. DON'T contact prospective contractors when a procurement is being solicited or offers are being evaluated.

am. DON'T assist prospective contractors in preparation of offers or quotations.

an. DON'T tell the contractor how to run his operation. This is his responsibility, and he is getting paid to manage.

ao. DON'T tell him to fire an individual. Terminations of employment are actions for the contractor.

ap. DON'T let personalities enter into your discussion with the contractor.

aq. DON'T request the contractor to do any work outside the scope of the contract.

ar. DON'T permit the contractor to proceed on his own on work outside the scope of the contract. It may be in the contractor's interests to exceed his contractual limitation with the intent of claiming additional consideration for additional effort. Coordinate immediately with the Contracting Officer.

as. DON'T commit the equipment, supplies, or personnel of the contractor for use by others. The contractor and the Contracting Officer control all such matters.

at. DON'T permit the contract to take on the appearance of a personal services contract; e.g., where the contractor personnel appear, in effect, to be Government employees. Do avoid any employee-employer relationship where Contractor personnel are subject to relatively continuous supervision and control by a Government employee. The contract determines what, how, and when the contractor does particular tasks (See Attachment 10).

au. DON'T you or any member or your family accept any gratuities. To be safe, don't accept any gifts, loans, or favors from a contractor or from their employees. Report any offers made immediately to the Contracting Officer.

av. DON'T accept an appointment as a COR if there is a potential conflict of interest. Report the matter immediately to your supervisor and the Contracting Officer for determination.

aw. DON'T accept a COR appointment if you do not have the time to perform a thorough and complete job of the duties in your Letter of Appointment and this handbook. On some types of contracts, performance as COR on even a few contracts may require substantially a full time effort.

ax. DON'T attest to having read and understood DoD 5500.7-R, Joint Ethics Regulation, without understanding the contents.

ay. DON'T ask to buy today what you needed yesterday - PLAN AHEAD.

az. DON'T negotiate or accept any offer of employment from a contractor related to your COR duties. Report any such discussion immediately to your supervisor, ethics counselor and the PCO.

SECTION XII: STANDARDS OF CONDUCT

Review of Standards

All Government personnel engaged in contracting and related activities must conduct business dealings with industry in a manner above reproach. They must also protect the U.S. Government's interests and maintain its reputation for fair dealings with contractors. DoD 5500.7-R, The Joint Ethics Regulation (JER), http://www.deskbook.osd.mil/ , sets forth applicable standards for contracting or related activities. All Contracting Officer's Representative (COR) letters of appointment require CORs to certify that they have read and understand the JER. In addition to the JER, CORs should be familiar with the Procurement Integrity Act, which is covered at FAR 3.104.

CORs who may have direct or indirect financial interests which would place the COR in a position where there is a conflict between the COR's private interests and the public interests of the United States shall advise their supervisor and the contracting officer of the conflict so that appropriate action may be taken. CORs shall avoid even the appearance of a conflict of interests in order to maintain public confidence in the U.S Government's conduct of business with the private sector. CORs must supply evidence to the Contracting Officer that she/he has officially filed a OGE Form 450 Confidential Financial Disclosure Report.

The JER sets forth the following Code of Ethics for Government Service, which all CORs are required to follow:

     a. Put loyalty to the highest moral principles and to country above loyalty to persons, party, or Government department.

     b. Uphold the Constitution, laws, and regulations of the United States and of all governments therein and never be a party to their evasion.

     c. Give a full day's labor for a full day's pay; giving earnest effort and best thought to the performance of duties.

     d. Seek to find and employ more efficient and economical ways of getting tasks accomplished.

     e. Never discriminate unfairly by the dispensing of special favors or privileges to anyone, whether for remuneration or not; and never accept, for himself or herself or for family members, favors or benefits under circumstances which might be construed by reasonable persons as influencing the performance of governmental duties

     f. Make no private promises of any kind binding upon the duties of office, since a Government employee has no private word that can be binding on public duty.

     g. Engage in no business with the Government, either directly or indirectly, which is inconsistent with the conscientious performance of governmental duties.

h. Never use any information gained confidentially in the performance of governmental duties as a means of making private profit.

    i. Expose corruption wherever discovered.

    j. Uphold these principles, ever conscious that public office is a public trust.

Gratuities

CORs will not under any circumstances, solicit, accept, or agree to accept favors, gratuities, considerations, assistance, or entertainment offered to either the COR or members of the COR's family from any contractor or subcontractor contemplating doing business, or doing business with the Government

Protection of Pre-Proposal and Proposal Data

It is the individual responsibility of the COR to refrain from releasing to any individual, business establishment or its representatives any government information concerning proposed procurements. Such information will be released to all potential contractors as nearly simultaneously as possible, and only through the contracting officer, so that one potential officer may not be given an unfair advantage over another.

Proposal data submitted by contractors for evaluation under a government acquisition is competition sensitive and is often proprietary in nature. CORs who have access to proposals for evaluation and review are obligated to protect the data from release to third parties.

SECTION XIV - ATTACHMENTS

Attachment 1: Sample Contracting Officer's Representative Nomination Letter:

NOTE: THIS FORM IS IN THREE PARTS. ALL PARTS MUST BE COMPLETED
AND THE FORM SIGNED BY THE SUPERVISOR (OR HIGHER
AUTHORITY) OF THE NOMINEE.

PART I: NOMINATION OF INDIVIDUAL

The following individual is hereby nominated to perform the duties of Contracting
Officer's Representative (COR) on Contract Number: _____
Order Number: _____.

COR NAME: _____
COMPLETE ADDRESS with zip code & OFFICE SYMBOL: _____
TELEPHONE NUMBER: _____ DSN: _____
KO: _____ Phone: _____

PART II: QUALIFICATIONS OF NOMINEE

1. The above individual is familiar with pertinent contract clauses such as changes,
inspection and acceptance, Government-furnished property, termination, and the
concepts of excusable and non-excusable delays in contract performance. This
individual possesses the necessary ability to analyze, interpret, and evaluate factors
involved in contract administration. This individual has the technical and
administrative abilities and the required security clearance commensurate with the
proposed COR duties. The individual's integrity and adherence to the Standards of
Conduct DoD 5500.7-R, The Joint Ethics Regulation (JER) and the Procurement
Integrity Act (FAR 3.104) are above reproach. In addition, the nominee has the time
available to adequately perform such duties.

2. COR TRAINING COMPLETED	HOURS ATTENDED	DATE Day/Month/Year
40 Hr ALMC Resident	_____	_____
40 Hr Other Agency (ALMC Equivalent)	_____	_____
40 Hr Contractor (ALMC Equivalent)	_____	_____
4 Hour DAU COR Overview Course	_____	_____
8 Hour DAU COR with Mission Focus	_____	_____

No COR will be appointed if they only take the COR Overview and/or COR With A Mission Focus course.

_____Note 2: (Check if applicable) The Nominee is currently attending one of the above 40 hour courses. I will notify the Contracting Officer by Memorandum immediately upon completion of training scheduled for _____. (Day/Month/Year)

Submit an electronic pdf copy of the completion certificate immediately, upon availability, to the Procuring Contracting Officer (PCO), the G-3/5/7 Training and Programs Division.

3. PREVIOUS COR EXPERIENCE ON MOST RECENT CONTRACTS:

CONTR No.   CONTRACTOR/ADDRESS CONTRACT TYPE   PCO/Phone

a.
b.

Current contract(s) for which nominee is performing COR duties:

CONTR No.   CONTRACTOR/ADDRESS CONTRACT TYPE   PCO/Phone

a.
b.

Percentage of time currently spent performing COR duties:_____

PART III   CERTIFICATION FOR NOMINATION OF COR – DoD 5500.7-R (JER) states the basis for determining the need for filing OGE 450, Confidential Financial Disclosure Report. Supervisor (or higher authority) of nominees for COR are required to certify that the nominee is in compliance with DoD 5500.7-R and the Procurement Integrity Act (FAR 3.104), as follows:

I certify that I am the Supervisor (or higher authority) of _____ and that:

_____This employee will complete the Monthly COR Report and forward a copy of said report to the PCO each month.

_____This employee has filed an OGE Form 450 and there is no conflict of interest or apparent conflict of interest interfering with this appointment. The employee will be required to file an OGE Form 450 each February for the duration of this appointment and notify the PCO of this using the February COR Monthly Report.

_____This employee will complete the 8 hour online Defense Acquisition University COR Refresher Training entitled COR With A Mission Focus by February of each year at www.dau.com and provide confirmation of completion in the February COR Monthly Report to the PCO.

Signature of the COR's Supervisor (or higher authority)

Attachment 2 : Sample Contracting Officer's Representative Appointment Letter

CONTRACTING OFFICER'S REPRESENTATIVE

APPOINTMENT LETTER
(AFARS 5153.9001)

(Use official letterhead and follow standard procedures for correspondence. ADDRESS THE DESIGNATION TO THE INDIVIDUAL BY NAME including rank or grade, and full mailing address.)

SUBJECT: Designation of Contracting Officer's Representative (COR) for Contract_____ (Enter number).

1. Mr./Ms. _____ , Pursuant to DFARS 201.602-2, you are designated as the contracting officer's representative (COR) in administration of the following contract:

Contract Number:

For: (Enter item/system/services.)

Contractor:

Contract Period:

2. You are authorized by this designation to take action with respect to the following:

a. Verify that the contractor performs the technical requirements of the contract in accordance with the contract terms, conditions and specifications. Specific emphasis should be placed on the quality provisions, for both adherence to the contract provisions and to the contractor's own quality control program.

b. Perform, or cause to be performed, inspections necessary in connection with paragraph 2a and verify that the contractor has corrected all deficiencies. Perform acceptance for the Government of services performed under this contract.

c. Maintain liaison and direct communications with the contractor. Written communications with the contractor and other documents pertaining to the contract shall be signed as "Contracting Officer's Representative" and a copy shall be furnished to the contracting officer.

d. Monitor the contractor's performance, notify the contractor of deficiencies observed during surveillance and direct appropriate action to effect correction. Record and report to the contracting officer incidents of faulty or nonconforming work, delays or problems. In addition, you are required to submit a monthly report concerning performance of services rendered under this contract.

e. Coordinate site entry for contractor personnel, and insure that any Government-furnished property is available when required.

3. You are not empowered to award, agree to or sign any contract (including delivery orders) or contract modification or in any way to obligate the payment of money by the Government. You may not take any action that may affect contract or delivery order schedules, funds or scope. All contractual agreements, commitments or modifications that involve price, quantity, quality, delivery schedules or other terms and conditions of the contract must be made by the Contracting Officer. You may be personally liable for unauthorized acts. You may not re-delegate your COR authority.

4. This designation as a COR shall remain in effect through the life of the contract, unless sooner revoked in writing by the Contracting Officer or unless you are separated from Government service. If you are to be reassigned or to be separated from Government service, you must notify the Contracting Officer sufficiently in advance of reassignment or separation to permit timely selection and designation of a successor COR. If your designation is revoked for any reason before completion of this contract, turn your records over to the successor COR or obtain disposition instructions from the contracting officer.

5. It is mandatory that CORs supply the Contracting Officer with evidence that she/he has officially filed OGE Form 450 Confidential Financial Disclosure Report each year by February 15th. The CORs can provide this evidence by providing a statement that this yearly duty has been completed in the February monthly report that CORs are required to provide to the Contracting Officer. Note: The actual OGE Form 450 does not need to be provided to the respective Contracting Officer Center.

6. You are required to maintain adequate records to sufficiently describe the performance of your duties as a COR during the life of this contract and to dispose of such records as directed by the contracting officer. As a minimum, the COR file must contain the following:

     a. A copy of your letter of appointment from the contracting officer, a copy of any changes to that letter and a copy of any termination letter. A copy of your formal COR training, except for Contracting Officer CORs who may substitute a current, valid Contracting Officer Warrant, or personnel who may substitute a Waiver of COR Training Based Upon Experience For CORs Appointed Prior To 11/01/2005 signed by the Principal Assistant Responsible For Contracting (PARC).

     b. A copy of the contract or the appropriate part of the contract and all contract modifications.

     c. A copy of the applicable quality assurance (QA) surveillance plan.

     d. All correspondence initiated by authorized representatives concerning performance of the contract.

     e. The names and position titles of individuals who serve on the contract administration team. The Contracting Officer must approve all those who serve on this team.

     f. A record of inspections performed and the results.

g. Memoranda for record or minutes of any pre-performance conferences.

h. Memoranda for record of minutes of any meetings and discussions with the contractor or others pertaining to the contract or contract performance.

i. Applicable laboratory test reports.

j. Records relating to the contractor's quality control system and plan and the results of the quality control effort.

k. A copy of the surveillance schedule.

l. Documentation pertaining to your acceptance of performance of services, including reports and other data. (See Attachment - Processing Contractor's Invoices)

6. At the time of contract completion, you will forward all records to the contracting officer for retention in the contract files.

7. All personnel engaged in contracting and related activities shall conduct business dealings with industry in a manner above reproach in every aspect and shall protect the U.S. Government's interests, as well as maintain its reputation for fair and equal dealings with all contractors. DoD Directive 5500.7-R sets forth standards of conduct for all personnel directly and indirectly involved in contracting.

8. A COR who may have direct or indirect financial interests, which would place the COR in a position where there is a conflict between the CORs private interests and the public interests of the United States shall advise their supervisor and the Contracting Officer of the conflict so that appropriate actions may be taken. CORs shall avoid the appearance of a conflict of interests in order to maintain public confidence in the U.S. Government's conduct of business with the private sector. As stated in paragraph 5, CORs must supply the Contracting Officer with evidence that she/he has officially filed a OGE Form 450 Confidential Financial Disclosure Report each February. This information may be provided in the February Monthly COR Report.

9. If the COR is responsible for maintaining the ASC G-3/5/7 Contract Requirements Database to ensure contract information is updated monthly. This spreadsheet identifies contract period of performance timeframes, Continuing Service Agreement s timeframes, CORs and Contractor information.

10. You are required to acknowledge receipt of this designation on the duplicate copy and return it to the Contracting Officer. Your signature also serves as certification that you have read and understand the contents of DoD Directive 5500.7-R. The original copy of this designation should be retained for your file.

11. Pursuant to the Prompt Payment Act, FAR 32.905(f), and AR 37-1, you are required to forward correctly completed acceptance/receiving documents to the paying office designated in the contract no later than five (5) working days after receipt and acceptance of goods and/or services. Failure to supply any required acceptance/receiving documentation within this timeframe may subject the

Government to interest penalties and result in charge back of any interest paid to the requiring activity's operating funds. Furnish a copy of any signed acceptance/receiving documents to the Contracting Officer.

12. The COR must sign and return this appointment letter to the Contracting Officer within **3** working days of receipt. Failure to do so will result in notification to his/her supervisor which could result in revocation of the appointment. Also, CORs must notify the Contracting Officer immediately when leaving the site of the original COR designation.

13. Contracting Officers shall **provide copies** of the COR Appointment Letter, the Certificate of Completion of a recognized 40 hour COR Course to the G-3/5/7 Training and Programs Division, AMSAS-OPS-T for tracking COR training requirements within 10 days of the COR appointment.

_____
Signature Block of Contracting Officer

Receipt of this Contracting Officer's Representative designation is acknowledged.

NAME:_____ (Print or type) SIGNATURE _____

TITLE: DATE:

RANK/GRADE: TELEPHONE:

CF:
Contracting Officer
Contractor
Requiring Activity
COR's Supervisor

Attachment 3 – Sample Termination Request Letter

<u>TERMINATION REQUEST LETTER</u>

(Office Symbol)

MEMORANDUM FOR (insert office symbol, name and "Contracting Officer")

SUBJECT: Request for Termination of Contracting Officer's Representative (COR) Designation

1. Due to my transfer from my position (or for whatever reason), request my designation as COR be terminated effective <u>(date)</u> for the following contracts:

CONTRACT NUMBER	CONTRACTOR
_____	_____
_____	_____
_____	_____

2. My successor will be   <u>(name)</u>   , extension <u>(number)</u>.   Enclosed is the certification for nomination signed by the Supervisor and a copy of the certificate for completion of training for the new nominee.

3. Point of contact for this request is   <u>(name)</u>   , extension <u>(number)</u>.

Encl 1   Name
                                                         Contracting Officer Representative
CF:
Contractor
Cognizant DCMA
Requiring Activity

<u>NOTE:</u>   Use this format for personnel transfer

Attachment 4 – Format for Monthly COR Report to PCO

<u>MONTHLY COR REPORT TO PCO</u>

Date_____

(NOTE: This sample is FOR YOUR INFORMATION ONLY. The Contracting Officer will attach a tailored report to your Letter of Appointment. If not attached, request one.)

CONTRACT NUMBER_____

SUPPLY/SERVICE_____

CONTRACTOR'S NAME_____

ADDRESS_____

TELEPHONE NO._____

NAME AND TELEPHONE NUMBER OF PCO_____

NAME and TELEPHONE NUMBER OF COR_____

Do you have available and have maintained current for inspection by the PCO a separate COR file for this contract containing a copy of the contract and all modifications, your appointment, copies of trip reports for all visits/meetings, copies of all correspondence between you and the contractor, etc.? (If the answer is NO, call your PCO.) YES_____ NO_____

Attach copies or trip reports, minutes of meeting and correspondence not already furnished to the PCO.

<u>MENU OF QUESTIONS FOR REPORT</u>

Is the contractor performing in a satisfactory manner from technical, cost and schedule points of view? List any issues with the contractor's performance as they relate to:

a. Technical

b. Cost

c. Schedule

(Use attachments as necessary.)

What specific surveillance have you conducted during the month as to the contractor's prudent use of materials and labor to assure inefficient or wasteful methods are not used?

This is a time-and-material/labor hour contract. Have you done floor checks of contractor's time cards, reviewed labor, materials, equipment purchased/used by the contractor? YES_____NO_____ If No, explain.

Is labor, materials, equipment in accordance with the terms of the contract? YES_____   NO_____   If NO, explain.

Is use of labor, and purchase and use of material and equipment such as to preclude wasteful or inefficient costs to the Government?
YES_____NO_____   If No, explain.

Were any items, technical reports. services delivered and accepted during the reporting period?   YES_____   NO_____

Were any inventions first conceived and/or reduced to practice by the contractor during the reporting period? YES_____   NO_____   if YES. explain.

Was any Government-furnished property/material contractually required to be delivered to the contractor during the reporting period?
YES_____NO_____

If YES, was it delivered on time and per contract terms?
YES_____NO_____   If NO, explain.

Is a final technical report due under the contract during the reporting period?
YES_____NO_____

If YES, was It delivered per contract requirements?   YES_____NO_____
if NO, explain.

This paragraph is to be added each October:
I have signed and filed the required OGE 450, Confidential Financial Disclosure
Report by October 31st of this year.   YES_____NO_____

Is there any other matter concerning the contract/contractor under your cognizance
as COR (see list of duties in your COR appointment letter) that needs to be surfaced to
the PC0 applicable to this reporting period?
YES_____NO_____   If YES, explain.

Do you have any questions for the PCO applicable to your COR duties
during this reporting period?   YES_____NO_____   List if answer is YES.

                                        Signed:

                                        Date:
                                        COR

DISTRIBUTION:
Original to PCO
Copy to COR File

43

Attachment 5 – Sample Revocation Letter

REVOCATION LETTER
(On Letterhead)

MEMORANDUM FOR: Mr. John Doe, ATTN: (Office Symbol) address.

SUBJECT': Revocation of Designation of Contracting Officer's Representative (COR) for Contract No.(s)_____,_____,_____,

1. In accordance with AFARS 5153.9001, Para 4, your designation as the Contracting Officer's Representative (COR) in administration of Subject Contract(s) is hereby revoked. This termination of your COR responsibilities is effective_____ (date)____. Upon that date, you shall transfer all of your records to the successor COR.

2. Any questions regarding the foregoing may be directed to me or Ms./Mr. _____ DSN____or Commercial No._____.

                                        Procuring Contracting Officer

Receipt of this revocation is acknowledged. (After signing, return original, keep copy)

NAME (Print or type):_____   SIGNATURE:_____

TITLE:_____   DATE:_____

RANK/GRADE:_____   TELEPHONE:_____

CF:
Contractor
Cognizant DCMA
Requiring Activity

Attachment 6 – Quality Assurance Surveillance Plan

QUALITY ASSURANCE SURVEILLANCE PLAN

1.0 SCOPE

The purpose of this surveillance plan is to provide the ASC Contracting for <u>XXX</u> with the procedures necessary to monitor the performance of the XXX Contract. It provides detailed methods for identifying, recording and reporting deficiencies observed in the program.

2.0 FUNCTIONS SURVEYED

The functions surveyed are Technical, Schedule, Management and Cost requirements of each of the task orders which are issued under the contract. Overall performance on a task order basis will be reviewed monthly between the Contracting Officer Representative (COR) and the Technical Expert and/or the task project leader. This contract is a indefinite delivery, indefinite quantity, time and material effort.

3.0 PROCEDURES:

3.1 INSPECTION

The work performed under this contract will be inspected by two methods, 100% inspection of deliverables and feedback from Government task leaders and/or Technical Experts on each of the task orders. The following paragraphs describe the inspection process for each of the general categories of technical, schedule, management and cost performance measured against the task orders.

3.1.1 TECHNICAL

Technical performance will be evaluated on a real time basis and reviewed monthly through meetings between the COR, the Technical Expert and/or task project manager.

The Monthly Status Report from the contractor will serve as the trigger for this meeting. The Government task project leader will provide comments to the COR by the last day of each month for discussion between the COR and the contractor Project Manager.

The technical elements monitored under this contract vary with each delivery order. Factors that may be evaluated and monitored are as follows:

- Anticipation of Issues
- Adaptability to Change
- Response Time
- Technical Complexity of Response

- Support & Product Quality

3.1.2 SCHEDULE

The contractors' schedule performance is reviewed and evaluated by the Government task project leader on a task-by-task basis. Each month the task project leader will provide input to the COR by means of comments to the monthly status report. These inputs will be collected, analyzed and reviewed by the COR and the contractor Project Manager in the aforementioned meeting.

Although each delivery order has unique schedule requirements, there are two sub-items that are common to all delivery orders, Adaptability to Change and Response Time.

Various documents, studies and reports will be required on an as needed basis. Any document or data delivery required will undergo 100% inspection. The data items will be inspected in accordance with the instructions in the delivery order. Various technical engineering support required under any study will be monitored via customer complaints and comments to the Monthly Status Report. The COR will be responsible for seeing that any complaints are resolved in a timely manner

3.1.3 MANAGEMENT

Coordination between the Government task project leader and the contractor task project leader will ensure mutual understanding of requirements. Contractor staffing will be judiciously and responsively implemented to maximize resource utilization to satisfy task requirements. The Government task project leader through periodic interface with the contractor team members shall conduct a 100% inspection of resources provided.

Each Government task project leader shall provide the COR, on a monthly basis, an assessment of the contractors' ability to plan and implement staffing changes and provide the correct quantity and quality of resources, if deemed necessary. The COR and the contractor Project Manager shall review management topics at the monthly meetings. The management topics will be discussed on a delivery order basis. The topics are staffing assignments, responsiveness to staffing requirements, availability and quality of personnel.

3.1.4 COST

Successful completion of tasks within specified cost ceilings is a result of the comprehensive working relationship established between the Government and the contractor task project leaders. Providing the best value support to each task is the goal of this relationship. The task project leaders will conduct periodic meetings to ensure task expenditures coincide with work performed. This proactive approach to cost control will ensure all task objectives are met or exceeded within established budgets.

The task project leaders will provide the COR with a monthly assessment of delivery order cost control. The COR will provide the contractor Project Manager with any concerns/comments. Delivery orders will be individually assessed on the effectiveness of control.

3.2 DOCUMENTS/REPORTING

A copy of the monthly status report shall be provided to the Contracting Officer. Issues and concerns that cannot be resolved at the working level or which impact on contractual requirements shall be reported to the Contracting Officer for resolution and contractual action.

Attachment 7 – Avoiding Personal Services Problems

AVOIDING PERSONAL SERVICES AND OTHER PROBLEMS ASSOCIATED WITH CONTRACTORS IN THE WORKPLACE

As we are all well aware, the emphasis upon downsizing the Government has led to an increase in the use of service contractors to support mission requirements. In this regard, it is of the utmost importance that Government personnel avoid violating the express prohibition against "personal services" contracts.

In order to avoid a personal services contract it is necessary to be able to recognize one. A personal services contract is a contract that, either by its express terms or as administered, makes contractor personnel appear to be Government employees. The Government is required to obtain its employees by direct hire under competitive appointment or other procedures established by the appropriate civil service laws. Obtaining personal services by contract, rather than by direct hire, circumvents these laws.

A personal services contract is characterized by the employer-employee relationship it creates between the Government and the contractor's personnel. Federal Acquisition Regulation (FAR) 37.104(c)(2) states that the key question in determining whether an employer-employee relationship is created between the Government and the contractor is: "Will the Government exercise relatively continuous supervision and control over the contractor personnel performing the contract?" Simply stated, although they may be working side-by-side, contractor employees cannot be supervised by Government personnel. An arms-length relationship must exist between the Government and its contractor employees. Additionally, contractor personnel cannot perform "inherently Governmental functions," that is, any functions which require the exercise of personal judgment and discretion on the part of a Government official. Work assignments and taskings must be issued by the Government's point of contact, usually the contracting officer or the contracting officers' representative, to the contractor's point of contact, not from a Government supervisor.

The FAR provides guidance to Contracting Officers with regard to avoiding personal services contracts. Foremost in that guidance is the requirement to obtain the review and opinion of legal counsel in doubtful cases. All employees, not only acquisition personnel, should seek advice from legal counsel when confronted with a situation they feel may be a violation of the prohibition against personal services.

Perhaps the contracted function that causes the most controversy is that of contractor employees performing clerical/administrative support services. Most often, the contractor performs these services on-site; using Government furnished facilities, equipment and supplies. As a result of the proximity of the parties and human nature, the arms-length relationship between Government personnel and the contractor is sometimes diminished to the point that contract performance is converted from non-personal to personal in nature. A contractor secretary, administrative clerk or key entry operator should not be given direction, receive assignments from or be supervised by Federal employees. The fact that the Government has limited resources is not a valid reason for using contractor personnel to perform personal services or for Government officials to treat contractor personnel as Government employees.

The following are actual, real-life situations that have occurred at Fort Monmouth and/or within the Federal Government that have been determined to be violations of the prohibition against personal services. Please remember that the list is not intended to be all-inclusive, but rather merely representative of circumstances where a personal services relationship was created by the actions of the Government and contractor personnel:

• During a three-month period of time, the Government issued six hundred task orders to a support service contractor. This equates to one task order being issued every hour! Clearly, in this case, the Government was exercising continuous supervision and control over the contractor's employees. Hence a prohibited personal services relationship was created by the manner in which the Government administered the contract. Additionally, it is apparent that the Government misused the task ordering process established in the contract.

• A contract for what was purported to be stenographic reporting services was, in fact, a contract for secretarial work performed under Government supervision (in order to overcome a shortage of funds and personnel). The GAO determined that the contract as performed was for personal services and that the work should have been accomplished by Government personnel. Further, it was held that the Government could not make payment to the contractor for the unauthorized personal services performed under the contract. Accordingly, this situation also created the issue of whether the Government supervisor who ordered the work would be liable in his private capacity to pay the contractor for the (personal) services performed.

• A contractor secretary was required by a second-line Government supervisor to perform timekeeper duties for Government employees. This is a violation of the prohibition against personal services because the Government supervisor was exercising direction and control over the contractor's employee. Furthermore, the supervisor violated the Privacy Act by releasing protected personnel information to the contractor.

• At a Government test site, contractor personnel assisted in the testing of equipment. During a lull in the testing, the Government Test Director directed the contractor's employees to wash and wax the Government employees' POVs (figuring that the Government was paying for their time anyway). The Government supervisor created a personal services violation as well as contractual problems by directing the contractor to perform work outside the scope of the contract. His actions also created ethical and fiscal law problems because Government funds were improperly used to pay the contractor for cleaning privately owned vehicles.

- A PM requested a contractor to provide contract administration services, including issuing task orders and conducting negotiations on behalf of the Government. The contractor in this situation was being directed to perform inherently Governmental functions, that is, functions that require the exercise of discretion in applying Government authority, or the making of value judgments in making decisions for the Government. Only Government employees can properly perform these functions, hence this work cannot be contracted out.

- A contractor was improperly directed by a PM to purchase ADP equipment for the Government. This equipment was intended for use by Government employees in the normal course of their work and was to be included as part of the organization's property inventory. This function is inherently Governmental in nature, cannot be contracted out and must be performed by Government employees. Furthermore, the PM's actions circumvented the FAR requirements regarding competition and the proper procedures applicable to the acquisition of ADP equipment.

- A PM appointed a contractor employee to act as his agent and take actions on behalf of the Government regarding business matters, including the commitment of funds. Again, this was a situation where the contractor was being directed to perform inherently Governmental functions that cannot be contracted out.

As a direct result of the increase in the use of support services contracts, many more contractor personnel are now integrated with and work among Federal personnel at Government work sites. In addition to the personal services issues discussed above, this situation causes potential ethical problems that we must recognize and strive to avoid. The overriding principle that must be remembered is that contractor employees are not Government employees and should not be treated as such. In this respect we must recognize that it is common for varying degrees of relationships to develop in the workplace, ranging from acquaintances, to good friends, to intimate relationships, to marriage. When such relationships develop between Government personnel and contractor employees, we must be careful to maintain proper ethical behavior in the workplace and avoid even the appearance of unethical or improper conduct.

The following examples are representative of improper situations that have occurred as a result of contractors in the workplace:

- Contractor personnel and their workspace were not clearly identified; hence Government employees did not know that they were not Federal employees.

- Contractor employees did not identify themselves as such when attending meetings or answering Government telephones. To prevent the improper disclosure of procurement sensitive or proprietary information, Government personnel should always request meeting participants to identify themselves at the beginning of the meeting and ensure that they know with whom they are speaking on the telephone or during VTCs.

- Contractor badges were not clearly distinguishable from Government badges.

- Contractors were allowed to bill the Government for time that the Commander administratively determined to be non-work hours (i.e., participating in Organizational Day festivities).

- A contractor was directed by the Government to plan and set up an organization's picnic and holiday party. The contractor then billed the Government both for the work done as well as for the period of time the contractor employees were in attendance at these functions. Under no circumstances should contractor personnel be directed to and/or be reimbursed for organizing such functions. Nevertheless, depending upon the circumstances, it may be appropriate for contractor employees to attend these types of functions. In these situations, it is imperative that the matter be discussed with the Contracting Officer and legal counsel to determine if contractor attendance is proper.

- Contractor employees were solicited for contributions to gifts for departing and retiring Army employees.

- Government personnel did not require contractor employees to sign non-disclosure statements (to protect procurement sensitive and proprietary information).

Remember, the situations outlined above are not all-inclusive. Government personnel, particularly supervisors and Contracting Officers' Representatives, must guard against the temptation to utilize contractor employees in a manner as if they were in the civil service and be vigilant in avoiding problems which can arise as a result of having contractors in the workplace. Everyone is responsible and accountable for ensuring, especially in the administration of support service contracts, that they exercise the utmost care to both avoid the violation of the prohibition against personal services and comply with all other applicable contractual, ethical, fiscal and legal requirements.

If you have any questions or require any additional information regarding this subject, the contact your supporting contracting officer who will involve the ASC's Legal Office.

Attachment 8 – DA Memorandum, dated 17 AUG 99, SUBJECT - Contractors in the Government Workplace

DEPARTMENT OF THE ARMY
WASHINGTON, D.C. 20310
17 August 1999

MEMORANDUM FOR SEE DISTRIBUTION

SUBJECT: Contractors in the Government Workplace

This memorandum is to remind HQDA Principals and Army Commanders of their responsibilities relating to contractors in the workplace.

As Government functions are increasingly outsourced, making us more reliant on contractors, we must understand the advantages and limitations of using contractors, as well as the responsibilities associated with their use. Historically, contractors have successfully supported the U.S. Government during both war and peace, but who they really are and how they fit into an organization's operation is not always fully understood.

When properly used, contractors can assist Government managers in achieving their missions or enhancing their services. Contractors are managed through contracting channels based on the terms and conditions of the contract and the contracting officer's technical representative (COTR). The COTR assists in technically monitoring and administering the contract. Contractors are required to perform all tasks identified in the Statement of Work (SOW). However, contractors may not perform "inherently governmental functions." As a matter of policy, an "inherently governmental function" is one so intimately related to the public interest as to mandate performance by Government employees.

However, contractors may gather information or provide advice, opinions, recommendations, or ideas in these areas. They may develop draft policy and assist in planning and preparing budgets. In the contracting process, they may technically evaluate contract proposals, assist in developing SOWs, and serve as technical advisors to source selection boards. They may also participate as voting or nonvoting members of source evaluation boards. What they may not do is render a final decision. Nor will they supervise Government employees, make mission decisions, or represent the organization at policy decision group levels, particularly in financial matters.

To avoid any perception that a contractor is performing functions that are inherently governmental, Government managers should familiarize themselves with the Federal Acquisition Regulation and the relationship between Government personnel and contractors supporting their organization. Government and contractor personnel should also ensure that the work is related to a recognizable portion of the SOW.

When drafting service contracts, Government agencies will include a requirement that contractor personnel must identify themselves as contractors when attending meetings, answering Government telephones, or working in situations where their actions could be construed as official Government acts. The Government manager or COTR must ensure that the contracted employee displays his or her name and the name of the company while in the work area, wears and displays a building pass at all times, and includes the company's name in his or her email display. When a Government manager wishes to send a contractor to any type of meeting where classified or sensitive unclassified material may be presented, the COTR must provide-in writing or email-verification of the contractors' security clearance and/or need to know. Ultimately, the Government host who holds the classified or sensitive information is responsible for obtaining this information and ensuring that those who will receive the information have the appropriate security clearance and need to know before they admitted the contractor.

As stated previously, contractors do not supervise Government employees, nor do Government managers have direct control over contractor employees. However, the greater the degree of reliance on contractors, the greater the need for Government oversight. Therefore, HQDA Principals and Army Commanders must ensure that there are a sufficient number of experienced and trained government personnel available to exercise effective oversight of their programs that use contractor personnel. Ultimately, department heads and agencies are responsible for approving contracted work.

Finally, the Army policy is that sexual harassment and other forms of discrimination are unacceptable conduct in the Army workplace whether committed by or against its Government or contractors' employees. Violations of this policy could result in joint liability for both the Army and the contractor(s). HQDA Principals and Army Commanders are responsible for enforcing the Army policy.

Please ensure that this information receives wide dissemination. You may also find the following website helpful:
http://web.deskbook.osd.mil/default.asp?tasklist.asp.

//S//   //S//

John M. Pickler   Joel B. Hudson
Lieutenant General, USA   Administrative Assistant
Director of the Army Staff   to the Secretary of the Army

Attachment 9 – DFAS Vendor Pay Procedures

DFAS VENDOR PAY PROCEDURES

1. The Prompt Payment Act of 1982 requires prompt payment to contractors. The following financial tips will help expedite contract payment and will avoid interest penalties:

2. Financial Tips

   a. Vendor payments cannot be made without a proper acceptance.

   b. Receiving reports/acceptance service statements must be received at the DFAS paying office within 5 workdays after goods and services have been received and accepted.

   c. Promptly notify Contracting Officer Representatives (CORs) and receiving activities of changes to the contract's paying office.

   d. In accordance with DFAS-IN 37-100, the accounting classification must be complete and accurate on all funding and contractual documents. (CCR) Database.

   e. Ensure that vendors are registered in the Central Contractor Registration (CCR) Database.

   f. Remind vendors that Electronic Funds Transfer (EFT) is MANDATORY. DFAS will return invoices unpaid when contractor EFT information is not available.

   g. Ensure that contracts and/or invoices contain a tax identification number. (TIN).

   h. If your activity is the billing office, the vendor's invoice must be date-stamped upon receipt.

   i. Provide DFAS an E-Mail address for CORs and/or Points of Contact at receiving activities.

   j. Ensure obligations are recorded in the Accounting system.

   k. Ensure your activity's budget office and DFAS St. Louis have copies of your contractual documents.

   l. Be aware that shipping costs and freight must be obligated before a payment is made.

   m. Ensure receiving/acceptance reports contain (as a minimum) the following information:

 (1) Contract/Purchase order number
 (2) Description of supplies delivered or services performed to include the contract line number (CLIN)
 (3) Quantities of supplies or services received/performed
 (4) Date supplies/services were received/performed
 (5) Date supplies/services were accepted
 (6) Signature of Government official authorized to receive and/or accept supplies/services
 (7) Printed name, title, mailing address and telephone number of COR or designated receiving official
 (8) If the contract provides for the use of Government certified invoices in lieu of a separate receiving report, the invoice must contain the minimum information required on receiving reports

3. SUMMARY

Vendor pay interest penalties can be avoided if we ensure that contractual and receiving documentation:

 a. Are sent to DFAS vendor pay and budget offices promptly

 b. Contain accurate and complete financial data

 c. Are filled out correctly

 d. An obligation must be recorded into the financial system before a payment is made

4. REFERENCES:

DFAS, Financial Management Regulation DFAS-IN 37-1, CH 20*

The Army Management Structure DFAS-IN 37-100-99*

DFAS-IN Policy and Systems*

Central Contractor Registration**

---

*   http://asafm-www.army.pentagon.mil/dfas/default.htm
**   http://www.ccr2000.com
**   http://www.ccr.dlsc.dla.mil

Attachment 10 – COR Nomination & Appointment Process Flow

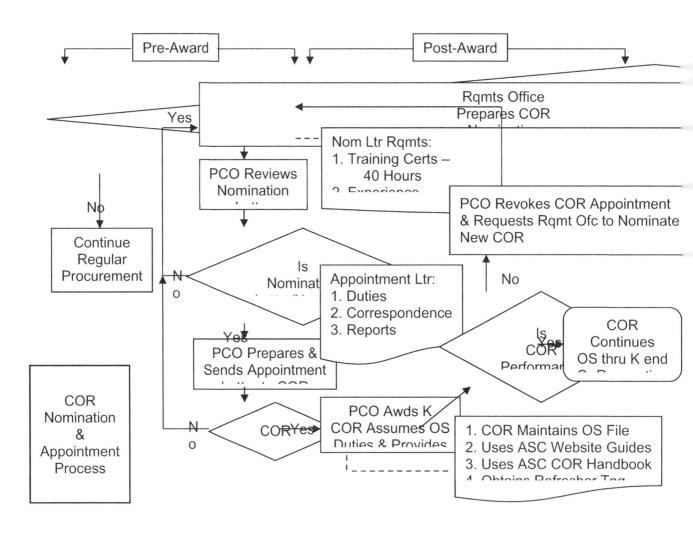

Attachment 11 - <u>ASC COR TRAINING REQUIREMENTS</u>

All CORs must complete the USA Logistics Management College's (ALMC) COR course or CLC 106 online at http://www.dau.mil/basedocs/continuouslearning.asp (or equivalent) before the contracting officer may issue a letter appointment. Information about the ALMC COR course is available at http://www.almc.army.mil/AMD/ALMC-CL/index.asp. Prior COR experience is not an acceptable substitute for the ALMC or equivalent training. Some commands require additional COR training, as well.

- The **ALMC COR course**, which is available in the following modes:

  - Resident at ALMC: One-week, in resident at Fort Lee, VA. Obtain course application and dates through your training representative.
  - On-Site ALMC: One-week on-site course taught by ALMC faculty, normally identical content to the resident course. Obtain course locations and dates through your training representative.
  - Satellite Education Network (SEN): Formal classroom instruction on-site using a live televised broadcast from ALMC, with a voice network to permit discussions between the instructor and the students. Contact your training representative for details.
  - On-Site ALMC Accredited Training: Formal classroom instruction on-site using course materials furnished by ALMC, with the local activity providing facilities and instructors. ALMC instructors may augment the team, when available. Contact your training representatives to find out about availability at your activity.
  - Equivalent Courses: Several contractors and other sources offer COR courses. If the contracting officer agrees to accept a course as a valid substitute for the mandatory training, contact your training representative to arrange for taking the course.

- **CORs must have a minimum of 40 hours of training; twenty-two of the required 40 hours of training hours must cover the essential COR competencies. The remaining 18 hours of the required 40 hours of training should include agency-specific courses, electives, and/or those identified by the COR's supervisor, in consultation with the Contracting Officer, as necessary, for managing a particular contract.**

- CORs should review training course material frequently, but no less than annually. CORs who manage large or complex contracts should consider taking the ALMC course or its equivalent every 3 years to maintain currency in COR practices.

- Continuous Learning: To maintain a FAC-COR, CORs **are required to earn 40 continuous learning points (CLPs) of skills currency training every two years beginning FY09.** The training can be obtained through FAI, the Defense Acquisition University, commercially available sources, colleges or universities, or agency-specific courses. ACMs, or designees, shall monitor the continuous learning requirements for employees holding FAC-CORs to ensure they meet this requirement. Additional guidance on determining continuous learning points is available on the FAI Web site at http://www.fai.gov/training/clo.asp

- A COR will expire **if the 40 CLPs are not earned every two years,** and the CAO, or other appropriate agency authority, shall recommend that the COR's delegation letter be revoked or modified if this condition is not met. The COR must be notified in writing in a timely manner of any changes to his or her delegation of authority, and the contractor should be notified as appropriate.

- CORs should take **refresher training of at least six (students choice of topics) of the 18 modules offered by the on-line Federal Acquisition Institute (FAI)** Mentor course available at http://www.fai.gov/.

Attachment 13 – COR Performance Objectives / Standards

PERFORMANCE OBJECTIVES/PERFORMANCE STANDARDS
ASC Contracting Officer's Representative (COR)

Provided below are standardized COR performance objectives that would be inserted into COR performance plans. **All CORs MUST HAVE the following COR performance objective put into their performance plan within 30 days of COR appointment.**

NSPS Job Objective – To be combined with another Job Objective. This should not be a stand alone NSPS Job Objective.

COR Execution and Compliance: Examine and execute COR policies, regulations and guidance ensuring accurate and consistent maintenance of COR records. Work product is clear and in accordance with law and regulation. Keep current on mandatory COR training and financial requirements.

Contributing factor: Technical Proficiency

TAPES Performance Standards

COR Execution and Compliance: Examine and execute COR policies, regulations and guidance ensuring accurate and consistent maintenance of COR records. Work product is clear and in accordance with law and regulation. Keep current on mandatory COR training and financial requirements.

Military Support Forms

COR Execution and Compliance: Examine and execute COR policies, regulations and guidance ensuring accurate and consistent maintenance of COR records. Work product is clear and in accordance with law and regulation. Perform accurate and timely oversight of contractor invoices (as applicable) and performance. Keep current on mandatory COR training and financial requirements.

SECTION XV: DEFINITIONS

Acquisition - Acquiring by contract, with appropriated funds, supplies or services (including construction) by and for the use of the Federal Government through purchase or lease, whether the supplies or services already exist or must be created, developed, demonstrated, and evaluated. (FAR 2.101.)

Administrative Contracting Officer (ACO) - A Contracting Officer who administers a contract and serves to enforce its provisions. A COR works very closely with this individual. The Procuring Contracting Officer (PCO) sometimes serves as the ACO especially for contracts performed on a Government installation.

Agent - An individual (agent) appointed by another party (principal) to enter into a business or contractual relationship with third parties. These relationships are legally binding on the principal and the third party. A contracting officer when signing a Government Contract does so as an agent of the U.S. Government.

Army Federal Acquisition Regulation Supplement (AFARs) – The Army's supplement to the FAR which outlines policy and procedures for Army organizations.

Change Order - A written order, signed by the contracting officer directing the contractor to make a change that the Changes clause authorizes. (FAR 43.101).

Contract - An agreement, enforceable by law, between two or more competent parties to do or not do something not prohibited by law for a legal consideration. FAR 2.101 defines a contract as a mutually binding legal relationship obligating the seller to furnish the supplies or services (including construction) and the buyer to pay for them.

Constructive Change - An oral or written act or omission by the Contracting Officer that is construed as having the same effect as a written change order.

Contracting Officer (KO) - An individual duly appointed with specific authority to enter into, administer and/or terminate contracts and make related determinations and findings on behalf of the U.S. Government. Only this individual can change the contract.

Contracting Officer's Representative (COR) also known as Contracting Officer's Technical Representative (COTR) - An individual designated by the Contracting Officer to act as his/her representative to assist in managing the contract. The authorities and limitations of a COR appointment are contained in the written letter of appointment. Regulatory guidance concerning designation, responsibility, and limitation of authority of the COR is in the Army Federal Acquisition Regulation Supplement (AFARS) Subpart 5153.9001 and DFARS 201.602-2.

Contract Specialist – Assists a contracting officer in the pre-award, negotiation, award, and administration of the contract.

Default - The omission or failure to perform a legal or contractual duty to observe a promise or discharge an obligation, or to perform an agreement.

Defense Contract Management Agency (DCMA) - A DoD agency that performs assigned preaward functions and post award functions related to the administration of Government contracts. Contracts performed on a Government installation are usually not assigned to DCMA for post-award management and must be administered by the Contracting Officer and the appointed COR.

Defense Federal Acquisition Regulation (DFARS) - The primary regulation that sets forth uniform policy and procedures for acquisition by all defense agencies.

Delivery Order - Any order for supplies (including construction) placed against an established contract or with Government sources of supply.

Delivery Order Contract - A contract for supplies that does not procure or specify a firm quantity of supplies (other than a minimum or maximum quantity) and that provides for the issuance of orders for the delivery of supplies during the period of the contract.

Disadvantaged Individuals - Persons who are economically or socially disadvantaged because of their race, sex, religion, or country of origin.

Employee - Employer Relationship – May exist under service contracts when contractor personnel are subject to the relatively continuous supervision and control of a Government officer or employee (see Personal Services Contract).

Federal Acquisition Regulation (FAR) - The primary regulation that sets forth uniform policy and procedures for acquisition by all executive agencies.

Information Resources - Refers to all resources and activities employed in the acquisition, development, collection, processing, integration, transmission, dissemination, distribution, use, retention, storage, retrieval, maintenance, access, disposal, security, and management of information. Information resources include doctrine, policy, data, equipment, and software applications and related personnel, services, facilities, and organizations

Information Technology (IT) - Refers to any equipment or interconnected system or subsystem of equipment, that is used in the automatic acquisition, storage, manipulation, management, movement, control, display, switching, interchange, transmission, or reception of data or information by the Army as an executive agency. IT includes computers, ancillary equipment, software, firmware, and similar procedures, services (including support services), and related resources.

IT embedded - IT embedded in or integral to weapon systems, machines, medical instrumentation, servomechanisms, training devices, or test and evaluation systems.

Firm Fixed Price Contract- An agreement to pay a specified price when the items or services called for by the contract have been delivered and accepted within a specified time.

Full and Open Competition - A procurement environment in which all responsible sources are permitted to compete.

Government Furnished Information (GFI) – That information which is in the possession of, or acquired by the Government and subsequently delivered or otherwise made available to the contractor.

Government Furnished Property (GFP) - That property which is in the possession of, or acquired by the Government and subsequently delivered or otherwise made available to the contractor.

Head of the Contracting Activity (HCA) - The official who has overall responsibility for managing the contracting activity.

Inspection - Examining supplies or services to determine whether they conform to contractual requirements.

Labor-Hour Contract - A labor-hour contract is a variation of the time-and-material contract, differing only in that materials are not supplied by the contractor (FAR 16.602).

 Labor Surplus Area - A geographical area identified by the Department of Labor as an area of concentrated unemployment or underemployment or an area of labor surplus.

Labor Surplus Area Concern - A concern that, together with its first-tier subcontractors, will perform substantially (at least 50 percent of the costs of manufacturing, production, or services) in labor surplus areas.

Legal Counsel - The Judge Advocate General or Staff Judge Advocate or civilian counsel providing legal services to the installation organization concerned.

Letter Contract - A written preliminary contractual instrument that authorizes the contractor to begin immediately manufacturing supplies or performing services (FAR 16.603-1).

May - Denotes the permissive (FAR 2.101).

Modification - Any written change in the terms of the contract.

Negotiation - Contracting through the use of either competitive or other than competitive proposals and discussions. Any contract awarded without using sealed bidding procedures is a negotiated contract. Negotiation may also be used to modify the contract after award.

Non-Personal Services Contract - A contract under which the personnel rendering the services are not subject, either by the contract's terms or by the manner of its administration, to the supervision and control usually prevailing in relationships between the Government and its employees.

Option - A unilateral right in a contract by which, for a specified time, the Government may elect to purchase additional supplies or services called for by the contract, or may elect to extend the term of the contract.

Organizational and Consultant Conflicts of Interest - A situation that exists when the nature of the work to be performed under a proposed Government contract, may without some restriction on future activities, result in an unfair competitive advantage to the contractor or impair the contractor's objectivity in performing the contract work (FAR 9.5).

Policy Acquisition Letter (PAL) -

Partial Payments - A payment method for supplies or services delivered to, and accepted by the Government, that represent only part of the contract requirements.

Personal Services Contract - A contract that by its express terms or as administered makes contractor personnel appear, in effect, to be Government employees.

Policy Alert (PA) -

Pre-Award Survey - An evaluation by a surveying activity of a prospective contractor's capability to perform a proposed contract.

Procurement Initiator (PI) - Local or installation director, office chief or functional element authorized to receive contract support.

Procurement Request - The initial request for any contracting action, submitted by the Procurement Initiator which consists of a Funding document and all the documentation required to establish a contract, or documentation required to establish a purchase order or construction contract.

Quality Assurance - Various functions, including inspection, performed by the Government to determine whether a contractor has fulfilled the contact obligations pertaining to quality and quantity.

Ratification - The act of approving an unauthorized commitment by an official who has the authority to do so. (FAR 1.602-3).

Regulations - DoD 5500.7-R, Joint Ethics Regulation (JER); FAR 3.104 Procurement Integrity Act; FAR 42.302 Contract Administration Functions; DFARS 242 Contract Administration

Sealed Bidding - A method of contracting that employs competitive bids, public opening of bids, and where award is made to the responsive, responsible bidder, considering only price, and price-related factors (FAR 14.1).

Shall - Denotes the imperative (FAR 2.101).

Small and Disadvantage Business Utilization Specialist (SADBUS) - A position created under the authority of the Small Business Act, 15 U.S.C.644(1), and which is responsible for: Overall management and direction of the DoD Small Business Program, advising on matters relating to these programs; providing guidance and periodically reviewing the direction and implementation of DoD activities in promoting contract awards of small business goals and consulting with the Small Business Administration regarding the establishment of such goals (DFARS 219.201).

Small Business - A business concern which, including its affiliates, is independently owned and operated, not dominant in the area of business in which it is bidding on Government contracts, and meets certain other size-standard criteria set by the Small Business Administration (FAR 19.001).

Small Business Program (SBP) - A program designed to assure that small businesses, small disadvantaged businesses, 8(a) firms, women-owned businesses, minority colleges, universities and institutions, and labor surplus area firms receive a fair share of DoD procurement dollars. In furtherance of economic objectives, various public laws and executive orders have designated that these groups be provided special opportunities in solicitation and award of federal contracts

Sole Source - A source that is characterized as the one and only source, regardless of the marketplace, possessing a unique and singularly available performance capability for the purpose of the contract award.

Sole Source Acquisition - A contract for the purchase of supplies or services that is entered into, or proposed to be entered into by an agency after soliciting and negotiating with only one source. Sole Source contracts require special approvals.

Military specifications and Standards - Performance specifications shall be used when purchasing new systems, major modifications, upgrades to current systems, and non-developmental and commercial items, for programs in any acquisition category. If it is not practicable to use a performance specification, a non-government standard shall be used. Since there will be cases when military specifications are needed to define an exact design solution because there is no acceptable non-governmental standard or because the use of a performance specification or non-governmental standard is not cost effective, the use of military specifications and standards is authorized as a last resort, with an appropriate waiver. Waivers for the use of military specifications and standards must be approved by the Milestone Decision Authority (as defined in DoD Instruction 5000.2) In the case of acquisition category ID programs, waivers may be granted by the Component Acquisition Executive, or a designee. Waivers for reprocurement of items already in the inventory are not required. Waivers may be made on a "class" or item basis for a period of time not to exceed two years.

Supplemental Agreement- A contract modification which is accomplished by the mutual action of the contracting officer and contractor. This is a bilateral agreement and must be executed by both the contractor and the contracting officer.

Surveillance Plan - A guide, which describes the contract monitoring methods in detail. It is written by the work statement writing team when the work statement is developed, and used by the COR in managing a contract. It is mandatory for Time and Material contracts. Simple delivery contracts do not require a Surveillance Plan.

Task Order Contract - means a contract for services that does not procure or specify a firm quantity of services (other than a minimum or maximum quantity) and that provides for the issuance of orders for the performance of tasks during the period of the contract.

Task Orders - Any number of instruments used to order services under a task order contract. Task orders are always written by the contracting officer, and when obligating funds, must be on a form prescribed by the Federal Acquisition Regulation or the DoD Supplement thereto. Task orders are made a part of the contract file and the COR file.

Termination - The cancellation of all or part of the work that has not been completed and accepted under a contract. It may, under specific circumstances, be for default of the contractor or for convenience of the Government (FAR 49).

Time and Material Contracts - Provides for acquiring supplies or services on the basis of (1) direct labor hours at specified fixed hourly rates that include wages, overhead, general and administrative expenses, and profit, and (2) materials at cost, including, if appropriate, material handling costs as part of material costs. A ceiling price is established which the contractor may not exceed. Substantial surveillance on the Government's part is required to insure that inefficient methods are not used (FAR 16.601).

Unauthorized Commitment - An agreement that is not binding solely because the Government representative who made it lacked the authority to enter into that agreement on behalf of the Government. This usually occurs when a contractor relies upon the apparent authority of a Government official who does not, in fact, have authority to obligate the Government contractually. Such actions must be ratified at very high levels. If the approval authority, in his discretion, does not ratify the unauthorized commitment, the person who caused it may be held personally and financially liable. Even if the action is ratified, the person who caused it may be subjected to administrative or other penalties. (See Ratification)

Army Sustainment Command

Contracting Officer Representative (COR) Folder

TABLE OF CONTENTS

TAB 1
COR Handbook

TAB 2
COR Process Flow

Tab 2 – COR Nomination & Appointment Process

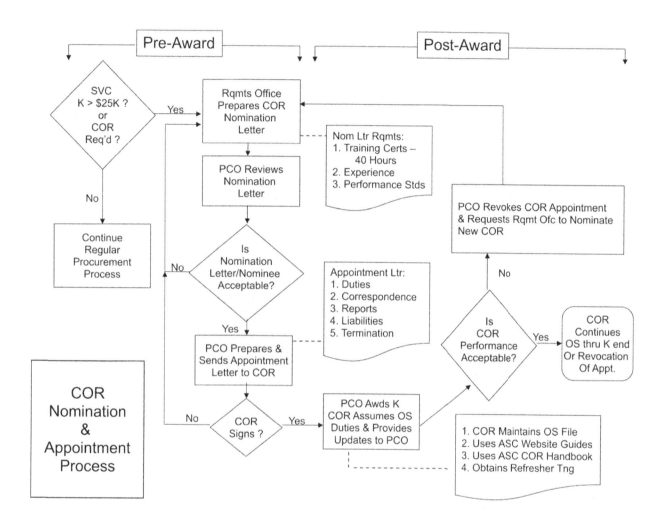

Pre-Award | **Post-Award**

SVC K > $25K ? or COR Req'd ?

— Yes → Rqmts Office Prepares COR Nomination Letter

— No → Continue Regular Procurement Process

Rqmts Office Prepares COR Nomination Letter → PCO Reviews Nomination Letter

Nom Ltr Rqmts:
1. Training Certs – 40 Hours
2. Experience
3. Performance Stds

PCO Reviews Nomination Letter → Is Nomination Letter/Nominee Acceptable?

No → (back to Rqmts Office)

Yes → PCO Prepares & Sends Appointment Letter to COR

Appointment Ltr:
1. Duties
2. Correspondence
3. Reports
4. Liabilities
5. Termination

PCO Prepares & Sends Appointment Letter to COR → COR Signs ?

No → (back)

Yes → PCO Awds K COR Assumes OS Duties & Provides Updates to PCO

1. COR Maintains OS File
2. Uses ASC Website Guides
3. Uses ASC COR Handbook
4. Obtains Refresher Tng

PCO Awds K COR Assumes OS Duties & Provides Updates to PCO → Is COR Performance Acceptable?

No → PCO Revokes COR Appointment & Requests Rqmt Ofc to Nominate New COR

Yes → COR Continues OS thru K end Or Revocation Of Appt.

COR Nomination & Appointment Process

TAB 3
Contact PWS

TAB 4
Contract Modifications

TAB 5
COR Nomination Letter

TAB 5: Sample Contracting Officer's Representative Nomination Letter:

NOTE: THIS FORM IS IN THREE PARTS. ALL PARTS MUST BE COMPLETED AND THE FORM SIGNED BY THE SUPERVISOR (OR HIGHER AUTHORITY) OF THE NOMINEE.

PART I: NOMINATION OF INDIVIDUAL

The following individual is hereby nominated to perform the duties of COR on Contract Number: _____ Order Number: _____.

COR NAME: _____
COMPLETE ADDRESS with zip code & OFFICE SYMBOL: _____
TELEPHONE NUMBER: _____ DSN: _____
KO: _____ Phone: _____

PART II: QUALIFICATIONS OF NOMINEE

1. The above individual is familiar with pertinent contract clauses such as changes, inspection and acceptance, Government-furnished property, termination, and the concepts of excusable and non-excusable delays in contract performance. This individual possesses the necessary ability to analyze, interpret, and evaluate factors involved in contract administration. This individual has the technical and administrative abilities and the required security clearance commensurate with the proposed COR duties. The individual's integrity and adherence to the Standards of Conduct DoD 5500.7-R, The Joint Ethics Regulation (JER) and the Procurement Integrity Act (FAR 3.104) are above reproach. In addition, the nominee has the time available to adequately perform such duties.

2. COR TRAINING COMPLETED	HOURS ATTENDED	DATE Day/Month/Year
40 Hr ALMC Resident	_____	_____
40 Hr Other Agency (ALMC Equivalent)	_____	_____
40 Hr Contractor (ALMC Equivalent)	_____	_____
4 Hour DAU COR Overview Course	_____	_____
8 Hour DAU COR with Mission Focus	_____	_____

No COR will be appointed if they take the COR Overview or COR With A Mission Focus course.

_____Note 2: (Check if applicable) The Nominee is currently attending one of the above 40 hour courses. I will notify the Contracting Officer by Memorandum immediately upon completion of training scheduled for _____. (Day/Month/Year)

Submit an electronic pdf copy of the completion certificate immediately, upon availability, to KO. The KO must provide an electronic pdf file to the G-3/5/7 Training and Programs Division.

3. PREVIOUS COR EXPERIENCE ON MOST RECENT CONTRACTS:

      CONTR No.   CONTRACTOR/ADDRESS CONTRACT TYPE   KO/Phone

     a.
     b.

Current contract(s) for which nominee is performing COR duties:

      CONTR No.   CONTRACTOR/ADDRESS CONTRACT TYPE   KO/Phone

     a.
     b.

Percentage of time currently spent performing COR duties:_____

PART III   CERTIFICATION FOR NOMINATION OF COR – DoD 5500.7-R (JER) states the basis for determining the need for filing OGE 450, Confidential Financial Disclosure Report. Supervisor (or higher authority) of nominees for COR are required to certify that the nominee is in compliance with
DoD 5500.7-R and the Procurement Integrity Act (FAR 3.104), as follows:

   I certify that I am the Supervisor (or higher authority) of _____
and that:

_____This employee will complete the Monthly COR Report and forward a copy of said report to the KO each month.

_____This employee has filed an OGE Form 450 and there is no conflict of interest or apparent conflict of interest interfering with this appointment. The employee will be required to file an OGE Form 450 each February for the duration of this appointment and notify the KO of this using the February COR Monthly Report.

_____This employee will complete the 8 hour online Defense Acquisition University COR Refresher Training entitled COR With A Mission Focus by February of each year at www.dau.com and provide conformation of completion in the February COR Monthly Report to the KO.

                  Signature of the COR's Supervisor (or higher authority)

TAB 6
COR Appointment Letter

Tab 6: Sample Contracting Officer's Representative Appointment Letter

CONTRACTING OFFICER'S REPRESENTATIVE

APPOINTMENT LETTER
(AFARS 5153.9001)

(Use official letterhead and follow standard procedures for correspondence. ADDRESS THE DESIGNATION TO THE INDIVIDUAL BY NAME including rank or grade, and full mailing address.)

SUBJECT: Designation of Contracting Officer's Representative (COR) for Contract_____ (Enter number).

1. Mr./Ms. _____ , Pursuant to DFARS 201.602-2, you are designated as the contracting officer's representative (COR) in administration of the following contract:

Contract Number:

For: (Enter item/system/services.)

Contractor:

Contract Period:

2. You are authorized by this designation to take action with respect to the following:

a. Verify that the contractor performs the technical requirements of the contract in accordance with the contract terms, conditions and specifications. Specific emphasis should be placed on the quality provisions, for both adherence to the contract provisions and to the contractor's own quality control program.

b. Perform, or cause to be performed, inspections necessary in connection with paragraph 2a and verify that the contractor has corrected all deficiencies. Perform acceptance for the Government of services performed under this contract.

c. Maintain liaison and direct communications with the contractor. Written communications with the contractor and other documents pertaining to the contract shall be signed as "Contracting Officer's Representative" and a copy shall be furnished to the contracting officer.

d. Monitor the contractor's performance, notify the contractor of deficiencies observed during surveillance and direct appropriate action to effect correction. Record and report to the contracting officer incidents of faulty or nonconforming work, delays or problems. In addition, you are required to submit a monthly report concerning performance of services rendered under this contract.

e. Coordinate site entry for contractor personnel, and insure that any Government-furnished property is available when required.

3. You are not empowered to award, agree to or sign any contract (including delivery orders) or contract modification or in any way to obligate the payment of money by the Government. You may not take any action that may affect contract or delivery order schedules, funds or scope. All contractual agreements, commitments or modifications that involve price, quantity, quality, delivery schedules or other terms and conditions of the contract must be made by the contracting officer. You may be personally liable for unauthorized acts. You may not re-delegate your COR authority.

4. This designation as a COR shall remain in effect through the life of the contract, unless sooner revoked in writing by the contracting officer or unless you are separated from Government service. If you are to be reassigned or to be separated from Government service, you must notify the contracting officer sufficiently in advance of reassignment or separation to permit timely selection and designation of a successor COR. If your designation is revoked for any reason before completion of this contract, turn your records over to the successor COR or obtain disposition instructions from the contracting officer.

5. It is mandatory that CORs supply the Contracting Officer with evidence that she/he has officially filed OGE Form 450 Confidential Financial Disclosure Report each year by February 15th. The CORs can provide this evidence by providing a statement that this yearly duty has been completed in the February monthly report that CORs are required to provide to the KO. Note: The actual OGE Form 450 does not need to be provided to the Acquisition Center KO .

6. You are required to maintain adequate records to sufficiently describe the performance of your duties as a COR during the life of this contract and to dispose of such records as directed by the contracting officer. As a minimum, the COR file must contain the following:

    a. A copy of your letter of appointment from the contracting officer, a copy of any changes to that letter and a copy of any termination letter. A copy of your formal COR training, except for Contracting Officer CORs who may substitute a current, valid Contracting Officer Warrant, or personnel who may substitute a Waiver of COR Training Based Upon Experience For CORs Appointed Prior To 11/01/2005 signed by the Principal Assistant Responsible For Contracting (PARC).

    b. A copy of the contract or the appropriate part of the contract and all contract modifications.

    c. A copy of the applicable quality assurance (QA) surveillance plan.

    d. All correspondence initiated by authorized representatives concerning performance of the contract.

    e. The names and position titles of individuals who serve on the contract administration team. The contracting officer must approve all those who serve on this team.

f. A record of inspections performed and the results.

g. Memoranda for record or minutes of any pre-performance conferences.

h. Memoranda for record of minutes of any meetings and discussions with the contractor or others pertaining to the contract or contract performance.

i. Applicable laboratory test reports.

j. Records relating to the contractor's quality control system and plan and the results of the quality control effort.

k. A copy of the surveillance schedule.

l. Documentation pertaining to your acceptance of performance of services, including reports and other data. (See Attachment - Processing Contractor's Invoices)

6. At the time of contract completion, you will forward all records to the contracting officer for retention in the contract files.

7. All personnel engaged in contracting and related activities shall conduct business dealings with industry in a manner above reproach in every aspect and shall protect the U.S. Government's interests, as well as maintain its reputation for fair and equal dealings with all contractors. DoD Directive 5500.7-R sets forth standards of conduct for all personnel directly and indirectly involved in contracting.

8. A COR who may have direct or indirect financial interests which would place the COR in a position where there is a conflict between the CORs private interests and the public interests of the United States shall advise the supervisor and the contracting officer of the conflict so that appropriate actions may be taken. CORs shall avoid the appearance of a conflict of interests in order to maintain public confidence in the U.S. Government's conduct of business with the private sector. CORs must supply the Contracting Officer with evidence that she/he has officially filed a OGE Form 450 Confidential Financial Disclosure Report each October. This information may be provided in the October Monthly COR Report.

9. If the COR is responsible for maintaining the ASC G-3/5/7 Requirements Database to ensure contract information is updated annually. This spreadsheet identifies contract period of performance timeframes, Continuing Service Agreement s timeframes, CORs and Contractor information.

10. You are required to acknowledge receipt of this designation on the duplicate copy and return it to the contracting officer. Your signature also serves as certification that you have read and understand the contents of DoD Directive 5500.7-R. The original copy of this designation should be retained for your file.

11. Pursuant to the Prompt Payment Act, FAR 32.905(f), and AR 37-1, you are required to forward correctly completed acceptance/receiving documents to the paying office designated in the contract no later than five (5) working days after receipt and acceptance of goods and/or services. Failure to supply any required

acceptance/receiving documentation within this timeframe may subject the Government to interest penalties and result in charge back of any interest paid to the requiring activity's operating funds. Furnish a <u>copy</u> of any signed acceptance/receiving documents to the Contracting Officer.

12. _The COR must sign and return this appointment letter to the Contracting Officer within **3** working days of receipt. Failure to do so will result in notification to his/her supervisor which could culminate in revocation of the appointment. Also, CORs must notify the Contracting Officer immediately when leaving the site of the original COR designation.

13. Contracting Officers shall **provide copies** of the COR Appointment Letter, the Certificate of Completion of a recognized 40 hour COR Course to the G-3/5/7 Training and Programs Division, AMSAS-OPS-T for tracking COR training requirements within 10 days of the COR appointment.

_____
Signature Block of Contracting Officer

Receipt of this Contracting Officer's Representative designation is acknowledged.

NAME:_____ (Print or type) SIGNATURE _____

TITLE: DATE:

RANK/GRADE: TELEPHONE:

CF:
Contracting Officer
Contractor
Requiring Activity
COR's Supervisor

TAB 7
OGE450 Completion Statement & Ethics Training Certificate/COR Training Certificate

TAB 8
NSPS/TAPES/Military/
COR Performance Objectives

Tab 8 – COR Performance Objectives / Standards

PERFORMANCE OBJECTIVES/PERFORMANCE STANDARDS
ASC Contracting Officer's Representative (COR)

Provided below are standardized COR performance objectives that would be inserted into COR performance plans. **All CORs MUST HAVE the following COR performance objective put into their performance plan within 30 days of COR appointment.**

NSPS Job Objective – To be combined with another Job Objective. This should not be a stand alone NSPS Job Objective.

COR Execution and Compliance: Examine and execute COR policies, regulations and guidance ensuring accurate and consistent maintenance of COR records. Work product is clear and in accordance with law and regulation. Keep current on mandatory COR training and financial requirements.

Contributing factor: Technical Proficiency

TAPES Performance Standards

COR Execution and Compliance: Examine and execute COR policies, regulations and guidance ensuring accurate and consistent maintenance of COR records. Work product is clear and in accordance with law and regulation. Keep current on mandatory COR training and financial requirements.

Military Support Forms

COR Execution and Compliance: Examine and execute COR policies, regulations and guidance ensuring accurate and consistent maintenance of COR records. Work product is clear and in accordance with law and regulation. Keep current on mandatory COR training and financial requirements.

TAB 9
Revocation/Termination
Letter

TAB 9 – Sample Revocation Letter

REVOCATION LETTER
(On Letterhead)

MEMORANDUM FOR: Mr. John Doe, ATTN: (Office Symbol) address.

SUBJECT': Revocation of Designation of Contracting Officer's Representative (COR) for Contract No.(s)_____,_____,_____,

1. In accordance with AFARS 5153.9001, Para 4, your designation as the Contracting Officer's Representative (COR) in administration of Subject Contract(s) is hereby revoked. This termination of your COR responsibilities is effective_____ (date)____. Upon that date, you shall transfer all of your records to the successor COR.

2. Any questions regarding the foregoing may be directed to me or Ms./Mr. _____ DSN____or Commercial No._____.

Procuring Contracting Officer

Receipt of this revocation is acknowledged. (After signing, return original, keep copy)

NAME (Print or type):_____   SIGNATURE:_____

TITLE:_____   DATE:_____

RANK/GRADE:_____   TELEPHONE:_____

CF:
Contractor
Cognizant DCMA
Requiring Activity

TAB 9 – Sample Termination Request Letter

TERMINATION REQUEST LETTER

(Office Symbol)

MEMORANDUM FOR (insert office symbol, name and "Contracting Officer")

SUBJECT: Request for Termination of Contracting Officer's Representative (COR) Designation

1. Due to my transfer from my position (or for whatever reason), request my designation as COR be terminated effective (date) for the following contracts:

CONTRACT NUMBER	CONTRACTOR
_____	_____
_____	_____
_____	_____

2. My successor will be   (name)   , extension   (number).   Enclosed is the certification for nomination signed by the Sector Chief (or higher authority) and a copy of the certificate for completion of training for the new nominee.

3. Point of contact for this request is   (name)   , extension (number).

Encl 1   Name
                                                    Contracting Officer Representative
CF:
Contractor
Cognizant DCMC
Requiring Activity

NOTE: Use this format for personnel transfer

TAB 10
Trip Reports

TAB 11
Monthly Reports to PCO

TAB 12
Memos/Correspondence to PCO

TAB 13
Memos/Correspondence to Contractor

Tab 13– DA Memorandum, dated 17 AUG 99, SUBJECT - Contractors in the Government Workplace

DEPARTMENT OF THE ARMY
WASHINGTON, D.C. 20310
17 August 1999

MEMORANDUM FOR SEE DISTRIBUTION

SUBJECT: Contractors in the Government Workplace

This memorandum is to remind HQDA Principals and Army Commanders of their responsibilities relating to contractors in the workplace.

As Government functions are increasingly outsourced, making us more reliant on contractors, we must understand the advantages and limitations of using contractors, as well as the responsibilities associated with their use. Historically, contractors have successfully supported the U.S. Government during both war and peace, but who they really are and how they fit into an organization's operation is not always fully understood.

When properly used, contractors can assist Government managers in achieving their missions or enhancing their services. Contractors are managed through contracting channels based on the terms and conditions of the contract and the contracting officer's technical representative (COTR). The COTR assists in technically monitoring and administering the contract. Contractors are required to perform all tasks identified in the Statement of Work (SOW). However, contractors may not perform "inherently governmental functions." As a matter of policy, an "inherently governmental function" is one so intimately related to the public interest as to mandate performance by Government employees.

However, contractors may gather information or provide advice, opinions, recommendations, or ideas in these areas. They may develop draft policy and assist in planning and preparing budgets. In the contracting process, they may technically evaluate contract proposals, assist in developing SOWs, and serve as technical advisors to source selection boards. They may also participate as voting or nonvoting members of source evaluation boards. What they may not do is render a final decision. Nor will they supervise Government employees, make mission decisions, or represent the organization at policy decision group levels, particularly in financial matters.

To avoid any perception that a contractor is performing functions that are inherently governmental, Government managers should familiarize themselves with the Federal Acquisition Regulation and the relationship between Government personnel and contractors supporting their organization. Government and contractor personnel should also ensure that the work is related to a recognizable portion of the SOW.

When drafting service contracts, Government agencies will include a requirement that contractor personnel must identify themselves as contractors when attending meetings, answering Government telephones, or working in situations where their actions could be construed as official Government acts. The Government manager or COTR must ensure that the contracted employee displays his or her name and the name of the company while in the work area, wears and displays a building pass at all times, and includes the company's name in his or her email display. When a Government manager wishes to send a contractor to any type of meeting where classified or sensitive unclassified material may be presented, the COTR must provide-in writing or email-verification of the contractors' security clearance and/or need to know. Ultimately, the Government host who holds the classified or sensitive information is responsible for obtaining this information and ensuring that those who will receive the information have the appropriate security clearance and need to know before they admitted the contractor.

As stated previously, contractors do not supervise Government employees, nor do Government managers have direct control over contractor employees. However, the greater the degree of reliance on contractors, the greater the need for Government oversight. Therefore, HQDA Principals and Army Commanders must ensure that there are a sufficient number of experienced and trained government personnel available to exercise effective oversight of their programs that use contractor personnel. Ultimately, department heads and agencies are responsible for approving contracted work.

Finally, the Army policy is that sexual harassment and other forms of discrimination are unacceptable conduct in the Army workplace whether committed by or against its Government or contractors' employees. Violations of this policy could result in joint liability for both the Army and the contractor(s). HQDA Principals and Army Commanders are responsible for enforcing the Army policy.

Please ensure that this information receives wide dissemination. You may also find the following website helpful:
http://web.deskbook.osd.mil/default.asp?tasklist.asp.

//S//   //S//

John M. Pickler   Joel B. Hudson
Lieutenant General, USA   Administrative Assistant
Director of the Army Staff   to the Secretary of the Army

TAB 14
QASP

TAB 15
Processed Invoices

Army Sustainment Command

Contracting Officer Representative (COR)

FORMS

MATERIAL INSPECTION AND RECEIVING REPORT

Form Approved
OMB No. 0704-0248

PLEASE DO NOT RETURN YOUR COMPLETED FORM TO THE ABOVE ORGANIZATION.
SEND THIS FORM IN ACCORDANCE WITH THE INSTRUCTIONS CONTAINED IN THE DFARS, APPENDIX F-401.

1. PROCUREMENT INSTRUMENT IDENTIFICATION (CONTRACT) NO.	ORDER NO.	6. INVOICE NO./DATE	7. PAGE	OF	8. ACCEPTANCE POINT

2. SHIPMENT NO.	3. DATE SHIPPED	4. B/L TCN	5. DISCOUNT TERMS

9. PRIME CONTRACTOR CODE	10. ADMINISTERED BY CODE

11. SHIPPED FROM (If other than 9) CODE	FOB:	12. PAYMENT WILL BE MADE BY CODE

13. SHIPPED TO CODE	14. MARKED FOR CODE

15. ITEM NO.	16. STOCK/PART NO. DESCRIPTION (Indicate number of shipping containers - type of container - container number.)	17. QUANTITY SHIP/REC'D*	18. UNIT	19. UNIT PRICE	20. AMOUNT

21. CONTRACT QUALITY ASSURANCE

a. ORIGIN

[ ] CQA   [ ] ACCEPTANCE of listed items has been made by me or under my supervision and they conform to contract, except as noted herein or on supporting documents.

DATE ___   SIGNATURE OF AUTHORIZED GOVERNMENT REPRESENTATIVE

TYPED NAME:

TITLE:

MAILING ADDRESS:

COMMERCIAL TELEPHONE NUMBER:

b. DESTINATION

[ ] CQA   [ ] ACCEPTANCE of listed items has been made by me or under my supervision and they conform to contract, except as noted herein or on supporting documents.

DATE ___   SIGNATURE OF AUTHORIZED GOVERNMENT REPRESENTATIVE

TYPED NAME:

TITLE:

MAILING ADDRESS:

COMMERCIAL TELEPHONE NUMBER:

22. RECEIVER'S USE

Quantities shown in column 17 were received in apparent good condition except as noted.

DATE RECEIVED ___   SIGNATURE OF AUTHORIZED GOVERNMENT REPRESENTATIVE

TYPED NAME:

TITLE:

MAILING ADDRESS:

COMMERCIAL TELEPHONE NUMBER:

* If quantity received by the Government is the same as quantity shipped, indicate by (X) mark; if different, enter actual quantity received below quantity shipped and encircle.

23. CONTRACTOR USE ONLY

97

DD FORM 250, AUG 2000   PREVIOUS EDITION IS OBSOLETE.   Adobe Professional 8.0

CONTRACT DISCREPANCY REPORT

1. CONTRACT NUMBER	2. REPORT NUMBER FOR THIS DISCREPANCY
3. TO *(Contractor and Manager's Name)*	4. FROM *(Name of QAE)*

5. DATES *(YYYYMMDD)*

a. PREPARED	b. RETURNED BY CONTRACTOR	c. ACTION COMPLETE

6. DISCREPANCY OR PROBLEM *(Describe in detail. Include reference to PWS Directive; attach continuation sheet if necessary.)*

7. SIGNATURE OF CONTRACTING OFFICER

8a. TO *(Contracting Officer)*	b. FROM *(Contractor)*

9. CONTRACTOR RESPONSE AS TO CAUSE, CORRECTIVE ACTION AND ACTIONS TO PREVENT RECURRENCE. *(Cite applicable Q.C. program procedures or new Q.C. procedures. Attach continuation sheet(s) if necessary.)*

10. SIGNATURE OF CONTRACTOR REPRESENTATIVE	b. DATE *(YYYYMMDD)*

11. GOVERNMENT EVALUATION *(Acceptance, partial acceptance, reflection. Attach continuation sheet(s) if necessary)*

12. GOVERNMENT ACTIONS *(Reduced payment, cure notice, show cause, other)*

13. CLOSE OUT

	NAME (1)	TITLE (2)	SIGNATURE (3)	DATE *(YYYYMMDD)* (4)
a. CONTRACTOR NOTIFIED				
b. QAE				
c. ACO				

DD FORM 2772, SEP 1998　　　REPLACES MT FORM 352-R, WHICH IS OBSOLETE.

LETTER OF AUTHORIZATION

			DATE OF REQUEST
			8/23/2007

REQUIRING ACTIVITY	GOVT AGENCY POC	GOVT AGENCY POC PHONE	GOVT AGENCY POC EMAIL
(e.g. Army Contracting Agency)	Doe, John	123-456-7890	lskdjsdjf@tst.com

NAME (Last, First, Middle Initial)	SSN / FIN	DATE OF BIRTH	PLACE OF BIRTH
Jones, Stanley	xxx-xx-1234	6/1/1960	

HOME ADDRESS	CITIZENSHIP	PASSPORT # / EXPIRATION
	United States	1234567890123 12/31/2010

	DEPLOYMENT PERIOD START	DEPLOYMENT PERIOD END
	Wednesday, August 01, 2007	Monday, September 01, 2008

EMAIL	THEATER EMAIL
sfdjsk@tst.com	test.data@us.army.mil

CLEARANCE LEVEL w/ AGENCY	CLEARANCE DATE (MM/DD/YYYY)	JOB TITLE	SUPERVISOR / MANAGER ☑
None	Monday, January 01, 0001	Action Officer	NON-SUPERVISOR / NON-MANAGER ☐

COMPANY (full name)	COMPANY POC	COMPANY POC TELEPHONE	COMPANY POC EMAIL
XYZ Company	Smith, Jane	123-456-7890	skdljk@tst.com

CONTRACT NUMBER/ TASK ORDER	CONTRACT PERIOD START	CONTRACT PERIOD END	CONTRACT ISSUING AGENCY
XYZ1234/ABC7890	12/12/2006	12/12/2012	(e.g. DARPA)

NEXT OF KIN (NOK) NAME	NOK RELATIONSHIP	NOK TELEPHONE	NOK ALTERNATE TELEPHONE

IN-THEATER CONTACT	CONTACT'S PHONE	CONTACT'S EMAIL
	029938023984298	skdflkjsdf@tst.com

COUNTRIES TO BE VISITED	GOVERNMENT FURNISHED SERVICES	
Belgium	☐ APO/FPA	☑ Authorized Weapon
	☑ Billeting	☑ CAC/ID Card
	☑ Commissary	☑ Dependents Authorized
PURPOSE	☑ DFACS	☐ DoDI Essential
Test data	☑ Excess Baggage	☑ Fuel Authorized
	☐ Medical/Dental	☑ Mil Banking
FUND CITE w/ BILLING ADDRESS	☑ Mil Clothing	☑ Mil Exchange
Fund Cite	☐ Mil Issued Equip	☐ Milair
Fund Address,	☑ MWR	☑ Transportation
fund City, 55848		
United States		

The government organization specified above, in its mission support capacity under the contract, authorizes the individual employee identified herein, to proceed to the location(s) listed for the designated deployment period set forth above. Non-supervisory positions shall be rated GS-12 or equivalent. Supervisory / Managerial positions shall be rated as GS-13 or equivalent. Upon completion of the mission, the employee will return to the point of origin. Travel being performed is necessary and in the public's service. Travel is in accordance with FAR 31.205-36 and the maximum per diem allowable under the appropriate travel regulations (Joint Travel Regulation (for AK, HI and outlying areas of the United States and US possessions), Federal Travel Regulation for CONUS and US Territories, and Dept of State's Standardized Regulations for OCONUS Foreign Areas designated by DOS).

Emergency medical support will be determined by the appropriate supported commander. Contractor authorization aboard military aircraft will be determined by the supported commander. Necessary identification badges will be determined and provided by the supported command.

This Contractor is considered as "Key Personnel, Government Civilian" in connection with "Non-Combatant Evacuation Orders" at the civil service grade indicated above.

SKL7RJ

LOA REMARKS

Contracting Officer

Signature	Digital or pen and ink
Print Name	Contracting Officer or designated representative
Email	govadmin-org@tst.gov
Date	Thursday, August 23, 2007
Phone	123-935-5196

COR Monthly Report to the Contracting Officer

1. CONTRACT NO / SERVICE.:

2. CONTRACT PERIOD OF PERFORMANCE

3. CONTRACTOR:

4. METHOD(S) OF SURVEILLANCE:

5. This document is in accordance with the Inspection of Services Clause FAR 52.246-4 or FAR 52.212-4(a) Inspections (for commercial contracts) and the Quality Assurance Surveillance Plan requirements.

6. Complete each of the following and provide detailed explanation. Attach additional documents if explanation is long or requires supporting evidence.

        a. Quality of Work: ( ) Exceptional   ( ) Very Good   ( ) Satisfactory

                              ( ) Marginal   ( ) Unsatisfactory

        b. Was the contractor's performance timely ( ) YES   ( ) NO

        c. Are there any significant issues that should be brought to the contracting officer's attention?
                    ( ) YES   ( ) NO

        d. Action being taken by contractor to correct discrepancies:
                    ( ) YES   ( ) NO Discrepancies this month

7. CUSTOMER COMPLAINTS
     a. Number of customer complaints:
     b. Number of VALID customer complaints:

8. ADDITIONAL COR COMMENTS

9. I hereby certify that services have been received and accepted.

CONTRACTING OFFICER'S REPRESENTATIVE SIGNATURE / DATE

(NOMINATION OF CONTRACTING OFFICER'S REPRESENTATIVE (COR)

MEMORANDUM FOR (*Contracting Officer*)   *Date*

SUBJECT: Nomination of Contracting Officer's Representative (COR)

1. Reference Procurement Package for the acquisition of (*identify service*) in support of (*identify using activity*).

2. This office has a requirement for (*describe services being procured in slightly more detail*). A procurement package for this acquisition (will be/has been) forwarded to your office. The requirements of the Performance Work Statement (PWS) included in the procurement package are such that the appointment of a Contracting Officer's Representative (COR) is required. I therefore nominate Mr./Ms. _____, of my office to serve as COR for the proposed contract.

3. *Mr./Ms.* _____ contact information is as follows:

   Full name: _____

   Full address (include Activity,   _____
   Office symbol, Street address
   and Bldg number)   _____

   Telephone number/FAX: _____
   Electronic Mail Address: _____

4. *Mr./Ms.* _____ successfully completed DAU Continuous Learning Module CLC 106 entitled "COR with a Mission Focus" on (*date*). A copy of the course completion certificate is attached (Enclosure).

5. *Address CLC 106 refresher training in this paragraph if the 3rd year anniversary of the course completion date will occur before the projected end of the proposed contract.*

6. Other pertinent training (*with completion dates*) that *Mr./Ms.* _____ has successfully completed is listed as follows (to include CLM 003, Ethics for AT&L workforce):

7. *Describe the technical capabilities/qualifications of Mr./Ms.* _____ *for the COR position addressing such factors as:*

   o *Current or previous COR experience(list by contract number, contract type, contractor name and period of assignment designated as COR) o On-the-job training experience, describe each work assignment and instruction provided and include date for each assignment*

o Demonstrated ability to analyze, interpret, evaluate and document factors in contract administration

o Knowledge, understanding and familiarity with government contracting processes, concepts and clauses.

o Sufficient time and resources to accomplish the duties, if the nominee is currently managing other workload commitments.

8. I certify that I am the supervisor of *Mr./Ms.* _____ and this employee has filed an OGE Form 450 with the appropriate Ethics Counselor on the anticipated COR duties. There is no conflict of interest or apparent conflict of interest interfering with the proposed designation.

9. I further certify that contract surveillance duties will be/are reflected in Mr./Ms. _____ annual performance standards.

10. If you require additional information regarding this action, please contact the undersigned at DSN XXX-XXXX, or COMM (XXX) XXX-XXXX, email _____.

Signature Block for Proposed COR's Supervisor

Enclosures
CLC 106 Course Completion Certificate
CLM 003 Ethics for AT&L Workforce

CONFIDENTIAL FINANCIAL DISCLOSURE REPORT
Executive Branch

Why Must I File?

The duties and responsibilities of your position require you to file the Confidential Financial Disclosure Report to avoid involvement in a real or apparent conflict of interest. The purpose of this report is to assist employees and their agencies in avoiding conflicts between official duties and private financial interests or affiliations. The information you provide will only be used for legitimate purposes, and will not be disclosed to any requesting person unless authorized by law. (See the Privacy Act Statement at the bottom of this page.) Please ensure that the information you provide is complete and accurate.

When Must I File?

New Entrants: The report is due within 30 days of your assuming a position designated for filing, unless your agency requests the report earlier or your agency grants you a filing extension.
Annual Filers: The report is due no later than February 15, unless your agency grants you a filing extension.

What is the Reporting Period?

New Entrants: Report the required information for the 12 months preceding your filing of this form.
Annual Filers: Report the required information for the preceding calendar year (January 1 – December 31).

What if I Have Questions?

If you have any questions about how to complete this form, please contact your ethics official or go to the Office of Government Ethics web site at www.oge.gov and select **OGE Form 450: Confidential Financial Disclosure Report** under **Forms Library.**

PENALTIES

Falsification of information or failure to file or report information required to be reported may subject you to disciplinary action by your employing agency or other authority. Knowing and willful falsification of information required to be reported may also subject you to criminal prosecution.

OGE Form 450, 5 CFR Part 2634, Subpart I
U.S. Office of Government Ethics (December 2011)
(Replaces June 2008 edition)

Form Approved
OMB No. 3209-0006

Date Received by Agency	Page Number

CONFIDENTIAL FINANCIAL DISCLOSURE REPORT
Executive Branch

Employee's Name (*Print last, first, middle initial*)	E-mail Address	
Position/Title		Grade
Agency	Branch/Unit and Address	
Work Phone	Reporting Status New Entrant ☐ Annual ☐	If New Entrant, Date of Appointment to Position (*mm/dd/yy*)

Check box if Special Government Employee (SGE) ☐	An SGE is an executive branch officer or employee who is retained, designated, appointed, or employed to perform temporary duties either on a full-time or intermittent basis, with or without compensation, for a period not to exceed 130 days during any consecutive 365-day period.

If an SGE, Mailing Address (*Number, Street, City, State, ZIP Code*)

Step 1:   Read the instructions for Parts I through V on the following pages.

Step 2:   For each statement below, check Yes or No to describe your situation.

I. I have reportable assets or sources of income for myself, my spouse, or my dependent children.	Yes ☐	No ☐
II. I have reportable liabilities (debts) for myself, my spouse, or my dependent children.	Yes ☐	No ☐
III. I have reportable outside positions for myself.	Yes ☐	No ☐
IV. I have reportable agreements or arrangements for myself.	Yes ☐	No ☐
NOTE: Statement V is for annual filers only. It does not apply to new entrants and SGEs. V. I have reportable gifts or travel reimbursements for myself, my spouse, or my dependent children.	Yes ☐	No ☐

Step 3:   If you selected Yes for any statement, you must describe the reportable interests that you have in the corresponding Part (I, II, III, IV, or V) of the form.

Step 4:   Sign and date the form.

Step 5:   Submit the completed form to your ethics office.

I certify that the statements I have made on this form and all attached statements are true, complete, and correct to the best of my knowledge.

Signature of Employee	Date (*mm/dd/yy*)

FOR REVIEWERS' USE ONLY:

On the basis of information contained in this report, I conclude that the filer is in compliance with applicable laws and regulations, except as noted in the "comments" box below.	
Signature and Title of Supervisor/Other Intermediate Reviewer (*if required by the agency*)	Date (*mm/dd/yy*)
E-mail Address	Phone Number
Signature and Title of Agency's Final Reviewing Official	Date (*mm/dd/yy*)

Comments of Reviewing Officials

(Check box if continued on additional page ☐)

Employee's Name (*Print last, first, middle initial)*	Page Number

Part I: Assets and Income

Report for Yourself, Spouse, and Dependent Child:	Do Not Report:

• Assets held for investment with a value greater than $1,000 at the end of the reporting period OR assets held for investment which produced more than $200 in income during the reporting period, including but not limited to:
  – Assets such as stocks, bonds, annuities, trust holdings, partnership interests, life insurance, investment real estate, or a privately-held trade or business
  – Sector mutual funds: those funds invested in a particular industry, business, or location such as ABC Electronics Fund or XYZ Canada Fund (report the <u>full</u> name of the fund, not just the general family fund name)
  – Holdings of retirement plans, such as 401(k)s or IRAs (list each holding except diversified mutual funds)
  – Holdings of investment life insurance
  – Holdings of variable annuities
  – Defined benefit pension plans provided by a former employer (include the name of the employer)
	• Federal Government retirement benefits
	• Thrift Savings Plan
	• Certificates of deposit, savings or checking accounts
	• Term life insurance
	• Money market mutual funds and money market accounts
	• Your personal residence, unless you rent it out
	• Diversified mutual funds, such as ABC Equity Value Fund or XYZ Large Capital Fund
	• U.S. Government Treasury bonds, bills, notes, and savings bonds
	• Money owed to you, your spouse, or dependent child by a spouse, parent, sibling, or child

Also Report:	Do Not Report:
• <u>For yourself</u>: (1) all sources of salary, fees, commissions, and other earned income greater than $200, (2) honoraria greater than $200, and (3) other non-investment income such as scholarships, prizes, and gambling income greater than $200 • <u>For your spouse</u>: (1) all sources of salary, fees, commissions, and other earned income greater than $1,000, and (2) honoraria greater than $200	• Dependent child's earned income • Veterans' benefits • Federal Government salary • Social Security benefits

Important Definitions

Diversified Mutual Fund – A mutual fund that does not have a stated policy of concentrating its investments in one industry, business, or single country other than the United States.
Sector Mutual Fund – A mutual fund that concentrates its investments in an industry, business, single country other than the United States, or bonds of a single state within the United States.
Dependent Child – A son, daughter, stepson or stepdaughter who is either unmarried and under age 21 and living in the filer's house, **or** considered dependent under the U.S. tax code.

Reportable Information – Go to the last page to see examples of how to report assets and income.

Specific stock, bond, sector mutual fund, type/location of real estate, etc. (*Indicate the full name of each specific asset or investment. You may add the ticker symbol to the full name.*) **Name of Employer or Business; Source of Fees, Commissions, or Honoraria** (*Include brief description.*) You may distinguish any entry for a family member by preceding it with S for spouse, DC for dependent child, or J for jointly held.	No longer held
1	☐
2	☐
3	☐
4	☐
5	☐

Employee's Name (*Print last, first, middle initial*)	Page Number

Part I: Assets and Income
Continuation Page

Specific stock, bond, sector mutual fund, type/location of real estate, etc. (*Indicate the full name of each specific asset or investment. You may add the ticker symbol to the full name.*) **Name of Employer or Business; Source of Fees, Commissions, or Honoraria** (*Include brief description.*) You may distinguish any entry for a family member by preceding it with S for spouse, DC for dependent child, or J for jointly held.	No longer held
1	☐
2	☐
3	☐
4	☐
5	☐
6	☐
7	☐
8	☐
9	☐
10	☐
11	☐
12	☐
13	☐
14	☐
15	☐
16	☐
17	☐
18	☐
19	☐
20	☐

Add Page

Employee's Name (*Print last, first, middle initial*)	Page Number

Part II: Liabilities

Report for Yourself, Spouse, and Dependent Child:	Do Not Report:
• A liability over $10,000 owed at any time during the reporting period, other than a loan from a financial institution or business entity granted on terms made available to the general public • A loan over $10,000 from an individual, such as a friend or a business associate	• Any liability, such as a mortgage, a student loan, or a credit card account, from a financial institution or business entity granted on terms made available to the general public • Loans secured by automobiles, household furniture, or appliances, unless the loan exceeds the purchase price of the item it secures • Liabilities that you owe to your spouse or to the parent, sibling, or child of you, your spouse, or your dependent child

Reportable Information – Go to the last page to see examples of how to report liabilities.

Name of creditor (*include city and state where creditor is located*)	Type of liability (*personal loan, margin account, etc.*)
1	
2	

Part III: Outside Positions

Report for Yourself:	Do Not Report:

• All positions outside the U.S. Government held at any time during the reporting period, whether or not you were compensated and whether or not you currently hold that position. Positions include an officer, director, employee, trustee, general partner, proprietor, representative, executor, or consultant of any of the following:
  – Corporation, partnership, trust, or other business entity
  – Non-profit or volunteer organization
  – Educational institution
	• Any position with a
	  – Religious entity
	  – Social entity
	  – Fraternal entity
	  – Political entity
	• Any position held by your spouse or dependent child
	• Any position that you hold as part of your official duties

Reportable Information – Go to the last page to see examples of how to report outside positions.

Organization (*include city and state where organization is located*)	Type of organization	Position	No longer held
1			☐
2			☐
3			☐
4			☐
5			☐
6			☐

Employee's Name (*Print last, first, middle initial*)	Page Number

Part IV: Agreements or Arrangements

Report Your Agreements or Arrangements for:	Do Not Report:
• Continuing participation in an employee pension or benefit plan maintained by a former employer • A leave of absence • Future employment, including date you accepted employment offer • Continuation of payment by a former employer (including severance payments)	• Any agreement or arrangement related to your employment by the Federal Government • Spouse's and dependent child's agreements or arrangements

Reportable Information – Go to the last page to see examples of how to report agreements and arrangements.

Entity with which you have an agreement or arrangement (*include city and state where entity is located*)	Terms of Agreement or Arrangement
1	
2	
3	
4	

Part V: Gifts and Travel Reimbursements

Fill out this part only if you are filing an Annual Report. If you are a new entrant or an SGE, skip this part.

Report for Yourself, Spouse, and Dependent Child:	Do Not Report:
• Travel-related reimbursements (items such as lodging, transportation, and food) totaling more than $350* from any one source during the reporting period; include where you traveled, the purpose, and date(s) of the trip • Any other gifts totaling more than $350* from any one source during the reporting period *If you received more than one gift from one source: 1. Determine the value of each item you received from that source 2. Ignore each item valued at $140 or less 3. Add the value of those items valued at more than $140; if the total is more than $350, then you must list those items on this form	• Anything received from relatives, the U.S. Government, D.C., state, or local governments • Bequests and other forms of inheritance • Gifts and travel reimbursements given to your agency in connection with your official travel • Gifts of hospitality (food, lodging, entertainment) at the donor's residence or personal premises • Anything received by your spouse or dependent child totally independent of their relationship to you

Reportable Information – Go to the last page to see examples of how to report gifts and travel reimbursements.

Source	Description
1	
2	
3	

Add Page

EXAMPLES

Part I: Assets and Income

Specific stock, bond, sector mutual fund, type/location of real estate, etc. *(Indicate the full name of each specific asset or investment. You may add the ticker symbol to the full name.)* **Name of Employer or Business; Source of Fees, Commissions, or Honoraria** *(Include brief description.)* You may distinguish any entry for a family member by preceding it with S for spouse, DC for dependent child, or J for jointly held.	No longer held
XYZ Japan Fund *(Example of sector mutual fund)*	☐
OGE Energy *(Example of stock that produced more than $200 in capital gains)*	☒
(S) OGC Communications *(Example of stock held in a 401(k) plan)*	☐
ABC Healthcare Fund *(Example of sector fund held in a variable annuity)*	☐
Rental Condo, Anchorage, AK *(Example of investment real estate)*	☐
Bryggadune University – former employer	☒
(S) Express Medical Clinic – employer	☐
Association of Accountants – honoraria	☐

Part II: Liabilities

Name of creditor *(city and state)*	Type of liability *(personal loan, margin account, etc.)*
John Jones (Denver, CO)	Personal loan from a friend
ANW Investment Company (San Francisco, CA)	Margin account

Part III: Outside Positions

Organization *(city and state)*	Type of organization	Position	No longer held
Bryggadune University (Memphis, TN)	Educational institution	Professor	☒
ISK Family Trust (Boynton Beach, FL)	Family Trust	Trustee	☐
Scenic Rivers Association (Nashville, TN)	Non-profit environmental organization	Member, Board of Directors	☒

Part IV: Agreements or Arrangements

Entity with which you have an agreement or arrangement *(include city and state where entity is located)*	Terms of Agreement or Arrangement
Dee, Jones & Smith (San Diego, CA)	Will receive pension benefits (defined benefit plan) *(Example of continuing participation in an employee pension or benefit plan by a former employer)*
Hartford & Brown (San Diego, CA)	Employment agreement with Hartford & Brown. Starting work as attorney in July 2012. Entered into agreement in October 2011. *(Example of agreement for future employment)*

Part V: Gifts and Travel Reimbursements

Source	Description
Dee, Jones & Smith	Leather briefcase *(Example of a gift totaling more than $350 from one source)*
CGH Culinary Institute	Airline ticket, hotel room, and meals incident to culinary seminar in Tokyo, Japan from May 1-5, 2011 *(Example of travel reimbursement)*

AWARD/CONTRACT	1. THIS CONTRACT IS A RATED ORDER UNDER DPAS (15 CFR 700) ▶	RATING	PAGE	OF	PAGES

2. CONTRACT (Proc. Inst. Indent.) NO.	3. EFFECTIVE DATE	4. REQUISITION/PURCHASE REQUEST/PROJECT NO.

5. ISSUED BY	CODE	6. ADMINISTERED BY (If other than Item 5)	CODE

7. NAME AND ADDRESS OF CONTRACTOR (No., street, county, State and ZIP Code)

8. DELIVERY

☐ FOB ORIGIN   ☐ OTHER (See below)

9. DISCOUNT FOR PROMPT PAYMENT

10. SUBMIT INVOICES (4 copies unless otherwise specified) TO THE ADDRESS SHOWN IN ▶ | ITEM

CODE | FACILITY CODE

11. SHIP TO/MARK FOR	CODE	12. PAYMENT WILL BE MADE BY	CODE

13. AUTHORITY FOR USING OTHER THAN FULL AND OPEN COMPETITION:	14. ACCOUNTING AND APPROPRIATION DATA
☐ 10 U.S.C. 2304(c)( ) ☐ 41 U.S.C. 253(c)( )	

15A. ITEM NO.	15B. SUPPLIES/SERVICES	15C. QUANTITY	15D. UNIT	15E. UNIT PRICE	15F. AMOUNT

15G. TOTAL AMOUNT OF CONTRACT ▶ | $

16. TABLE OF CONTENTS

(X)	SEC.	DESCRIPTION	PAGE(S)	(X)	SEC.	DESCRIPTION	PAGE(S)
		PART I - THE SCHEDULE				PART II - CONTRACT CLAUSES	
	A	SOLICITATION/CONTRACT FORM			I	CONTRACT CLAUSES	
	B	SUPPLIES OR SERVICES AND PRICES/COSTS				PART III - LIST OF DOCUMENTS, EXHIBITS AND OTHER ATTACH.	
	C	DESCRIPTION/SPECS./WORK STATEMENT			J	LIST OF ATTACHMENTS	
	D	PACKAGING AND MARKING				PART IV - REPRESENTATIONS AND INSTRUCTIONS	
	E	INSPECTION AND ACCEPTANCE			K	REPRESENTATIONS, CERTIFICATIONS AND OTHER STATEMENTS OF OFFERORS	
	F	DELIVERIES OR PERFORMANCE					
	G	CONTRACT ADMINISTRATION DATA			L	INSTRS., CONDS., AND NOTICES TO OFFERORS	
	H	SPECIAL CONTRACT REQUIREMENTS			M	EVALUATION FACTORS FOR AWARD	

CONTRACTING OFFICER WILL COMPLETE ITEM 17 (SEALED-BID OR NEGOTIATED PROCUREMENT) OR 18 (SEALED-BID PROCUREMENT) AS APPLICABLE

17. ☐ CONTRACTOR'S NEGOTIATED AGREEMENT (Contractor is required to sign this document and return _____ copies to issuing office.) Contractor agrees to furnish and deliver all items or perform all the services set forth or otherwise identified above and on any continuation sheets for the consideration stated herein. The rights and obligations of the parties to this contract shall be subject to and governed by the following documents: (a) this award/contract, (b) the solicitation, if any, and (c) such provisions, representations, certifications, and specifications, as are attached or incorporated by reference herein. (Attachments are listed herein.)	18. ☐ SEALED-BID AWARD (Contractor is not required to sign this document.) Your bid on Solicitation Number _____ including the additions or changes made by you which additions or changes are set forth in full above, is hereby accepted as to the terms listed above and on any continuation sheets. This award consummates the contract which consists of the following documents: (a) the Government's solicitation and your bid, and (b) this award/contract. No further contractual document is necessary. (Block 18 should be checked only when awarding a sealed-bid contract.)

19A. NAME AND TITLE OF SIGNER (Type or Print)	20A. NAME OF CONTRACTING OFFICER

19B. NAME OF CONTRACTOR	19C. DATE SIGNED	20B. UNITED STATES OF AMERICA	20C. DATE SIGNED
BY _____ (Signature of person authorized to sign)		BY _____ (Signature of Contracting Officer)	

AMENDMENT OF SOLICITATION/MODIFICATION OF CONTRACT

	1. CONTRACT ID CODE	PAGE	OF	PAGES

2. AMENDMENT/MODIFICATION NO.	3. EFFECTIVE DATE	4. REQUISITION/PURCHASE REQ. NO.	5. PROJECT NO. *(If applicable)*

6. ISSUED BY	CODE		7. ADMINISTERED BY *(If other than Item 6)*	CODE	

8. NAME AND ADDRESS OF CONTRACTOR *(No., street, county, State and ZIP Code)*		(X)	9A. AMENDMENT OF SOLICITATION NO.
			9B. DATED *(SEE ITEM 11)*
			10A. MODIFICATION OF CONTRACT/ORDER NO.
			10B. DATED *(SEE ITEM 13)*
CODE	FACILITY CODE		

11. THIS ITEM ONLY APPLIES TO AMENDMENTS OF SOLICITATIONS

☐ The above numbered solicitation is amended as set forth in Item 14. The hour and date specified for receipt of Offers ☐ is extended, ☐ is not extended.

Offers must acknowledge receipt of this amendment prior to the hour and date specified in the solicitation or as amended, by one of the following methods:
(a) By completing items 8 and 15, and returning _____ copies of the amendment; (b) By acknowledging receipt of this amendment on each copy of the offer submitted; or (c) By separate letter or telegram which includes a reference to the solicitation and amendment numbers. FAILURE OF YOUR ACKNOWLEDGMENT TO BE RECEIVED AT THE PLACE DESIGNATED FOR THE RECEIPT OF OFFERS PRIOR TO THE HOUR AND DATE SPECIFIED MAY RESULT IN REJECTION OF YOUR OFFER. If by virtue of this amendment your desire to change an offer already submitted, such change may be made by telegram or letter, provided each telegram or letter makes reference to the solicitation and this amendment, and is received prior to the opening hour and date specified.

12. ACCOUNTING AND APPROPRIATION DATA *(If required)*

13. THIS ITEM ONLY APPLIES TO MODIFICATION OF CONTRACTS/ORDERS.
IT MODIFIES THE CONTRACT/ORDER NO. AS DESCRIBED IN ITEM 14.

CHECK ONE	
☐	A. THIS CHANGE ORDER IS ISSUED PURSUANT TO: *(Specify authority)* THE CHANGES SET FORTH IN ITEM 14 ARE MADE IN THE CONTRACT ORDER NO. IN ITEM 10A.
☐	B. THE ABOVE NUMBERED CONTRACT/ORDER IS MODIFIED TO REFLECT THE ADMINISTRATIVE CHANGES *(such as changes in paying office, appropriation date, etc.)* SET FORTH IN ITEM 14, PURSUANT TO THE AUTHORITY OF FAR 43.103(b).
☐	C. THIS SUPPLEMENTAL AGREEMENT IS ENTERED INTO PURSUANT TO AUTHORITY OF:
☐	D. OTHER *(Specify type of modification and authority)*

E. IMPORTANT: Contractor ☐ is not, ☐ is required to sign this document and return _____ copies to the issuing office.

14. DESCRIPTION OF AMENDMENT/MODIFICATION *(Organized by UCF section headings, including solicitation/contract subject matter where feasible.)*

Except as provided herein, all terms and conditions of the document referenced in Item 9A or 10A, as heretofore changed, remains unchanged and in full force and effect.

15A. NAME AND TITLE OF SIGNER *(Type or print)*	16A. NAME AND TITLE OF CONTRACTING OFFICER *(Type or print)*
15B. CONTRACTOR/OFFEROR	15C. DATE SIGNED	16B. UNITED STATES OF AMERICA	16C. DATE SIGNED
(Signature of person authorized to sign)		*(Signature of Contracting Officer)*	

INSTRUCTIONS

Instructions for items other than those that are self-explanatory, are as follows:

(a) Item 1 (Contract ID Code). Insert the contract type identification code that appears in the title block of the contract being modified.

(b) Item 3 (Effective date).

(1) For a solicitation amendment, change order, or administrative change, the effective date shall be the issue date of the amendment, change order, or administrative change.

(2) For a supplemental agreement, the effective date shall be the date agreed to by the contracting parties.

(3) For a modification issued as an initial or confirming notice of termination for the convenience of the Government, the effective date and the modification number of the confirming notice shall be the same as the effective date and modification number of the initial notice.

(4) For a modification converting a termination for default to a termination for the convenience of the Government, the effective date shall be the same as the effective date of the termination for default.

(5) For a modification confirming the contacting officer's determination of the amount due in settlement of a contract termination, the effective date shall be the same as the effective date of the initial decision.

(c) Item 6 (Issued By). Insert the name and address of the issuing office. If applicable, insert the appropriate issuing office code in the code block.

(d) Item 8 (Name and Address of Contractor). For modifications to a contract or order, enter the contractor's name, address, and code as shown in the original contract or order, unless changed by this or a previous modification.

(e) Item 9, (Amendment of Solicitation No. - Dated), and 10, (Modification of Contract/Order No. - Dated). Check the appropriate box and in the corresponding blanks insert the number and date of the original solicitation, contract, or order.

(f) Item 12 (Accounting and Appropriation Data). When appropriate, indicate the impact of the modification on each affected accounting classification by inserting one of the following entries.

(1) Accounting classification ....
Net increase $ ....

(2) Accounting classification ....
Net decrease $ ....

NOTE: If there are changes to multiple accounting classifications that cannot be placed in block 12, insert an asterisk and the words "See continuation sheet".

(g) Item 13. Check the appropriate box to indicate the type of modification. Insert in the corresponding blank the authority under which the modification is issued. Check whether or not contractor must sign this document. (See FAR 43.103.)

(h) Item 14 (Description of Amendment/Modification).

(1) Organize amendments or modifications under the appropriate Uniform Contract Format (UCF) section headings from the applicable solicitation or contract. The UCF table of contents, however, shall not be set forth in this document

(2) Indicate the impact of the modification on the overall total contract price by inserting one of the following entries:

(i) Total contract price increased by $ ....

(ii) Total contract price decreased by $....................

(iii) Total contract price unchanged.

(3) State reason for modification.

(4) When removing, reinstating, or adding funds, identify the contract items and accounting classifications.

(5) When the SF 30 is used to reflect a determination by the contracting officer of the amount due in settlement of a contract terminated for the convenience of the Government, the entry in Item 14 of the modification may be limited to --

(i) A reference to the letter determination; and

(ii) A statement of the net amount determined to be due in settlement of the contract.

(6) Include subject matter or short title of solicitation/contract where feasible.

(i) Item 16B. The contracting officer's signature is not required on solicitation amendments. The contracting officer's signature is normally affixed last on supplemental agreements.

113

STANDARD FORM 30 (REV. 10-83) **BACK**

SOLICITATION, OFFER AND AWARD

1. THIS CONTRACT IS A RATED ORDER UNDER DPAS (15 CFR 7900)	▶	RATING	PAGE	OF	PAGES

2. CONTRACT NUMBER	3. SOLICITATION NUMBER	4. TYPE OF SOLICITATION	5. DATE ISSUED	6. REQUISITION/PURCHASE NUMBER
		☐ SEALED BID (IFB) ☐ NEGOTIATED (RFP)		

7. ISSUED BY	CODE		8. ADDRESS OFFER TO (If other than item 7)

NOTE: In sealed bid solicitations "offer" and "offeror" mean "bid" and "bidder".

SOLICITATION

9. Sealed offers in original and _____ copies for furnishings the supplies or services in the Schedule will be received at the place specified in item 8, or if hand carried, in the depository located in _____ until _____ local time _____

(Hour)   (Date)

CAUTION - LATE Submissions, Modifications, and Withdrawals: See Section L, Provision No. 52.214-7 or 52.215-1. All offers are subject to all terms and conditions contained in this solicitation.

10. FOR INFORMATION CALL: ▶	A. NAME	B. TELEPHONE (NO COLLECT CALLS)			C. E-MAIL ADDRESS
		AREA CODE	NUMBER	EXT.	

11. TABLE OF CONTENTS

(X)	SEC.	DESCRIPTION	PAGE(S)	(X)	SEC.	DESCRIPTION	PAGE(S)
		PART I - THE SCHEDULE				PART II - CONTRACT CLAUSES	
	A	SOLICITATION/CONTRACT FORM			I	CONTRACT CLAUSES	
	B	SUPPLIES OR SERVICES AND PRICES/COSTS				PART III - LIST OF DOCUMENTS, EXHIBITS AND OTHER ATTACH.	
	C	DESCRIPTION/SPECS./WORK STATEMENT			J	LIST OF ATTACHMENTS	
	D	PACKAGING AND MARKING				PART IV - REPRESENTATIONS AND INSTRUCTIONS	
	E	INSPECTION AND ACCEPTANCE			K	REPRESENTATIONS, CERTIFICATIONS AND OTHER STATEMENTS OF OFFERORS	
	F	DELIVERIES OR PERFORMANCE					
	G	CONTRACT ADMINISTRATION DATA			L	INSTRS., CONDS., AND NOTICES TO OFFERORS	
	H	SPECIAL CONTRACT REQUIREMENTS			M	EVALUATION FACTORS FOR AWARD	

OFFER (Must be fully completed by offeror)

NOTE: Item 12 does not apply if the solicitation includes the provisions at 52.214-16, Minimum Bid Acceptance Period.

12. In compliance with the above, the undersigned agrees, if this offer is accepted within _____ calendar days (60 calendar days unless a different period is inserted by the offeror) from the date for receipt of offers specified above, to furnish any or all items upon which prices are offered at the set opposite each item, delivered at the designated point(s), within the time specified in the schedule.

13. DISCOUNT FOR PROMPT PAYMENT (See Section I, Clause No. 52.232-8) ▶	10 CALENDAR DAYS (%)	20 CALENDAR DAYS (%)	30 CALENDAR DAYS (%)	CALENDAR DAYS(%)

14. ACKNOWLEDGMENT OF AMENDMENTS (The offeror acknowledges receipt of amendments to the SOLICITATION for offerors and related documents numbered and dated):	AMENDMENT NO.	DATE	AMENDMENT NO.	DATE

15A. NAME AND ADDRESS OF OFFER-OR	CODE		FACILITY		16. NAME AND THE TITLE OF PERSON AUTHORIZED TO SIGN OFFER (Type or print)

15B. TELEPHONE NUMBER			15C. CHECK IF REMITTANCE ADDRESS IS DIFFERENT FROM ABOVE - ENTER SUCH ADDRESS IN SCHEDULE. ☐	17. SIGNATURE	18. OFFER DATE
AREA CODE	NUMBER	EXT.			

AWARD (To be completed by Government)

19. ACCEPTED AS TO ITEMS	20. AMOUNT	21. ACCOUNTING AND APPROPRIATION

22. AUTHORITY FOR USING OTHER THAN FULL OPEN COMPETITION: ☐ 10 U.S.C. 2304 (c) ☐ 41 U.S.C. 253 (c)	23. SUBMIT INVOICES TO ADDRESS SHOWN IN (4 copies unless otherwise specified) ▶	ITEM

24. ADMINISTERED BY (If other than Item 7)	25. PAYMENT WILL BE MADE BY	CODE

26. NAME OF CONTRACTING OFFICER (Type or print)	27. UNITED STATES OF AMERICA (Signature of Contracting Officer)	28. AWARD DATE

IMPORTANT - Award will be made on this Form, or on Standard Form 26, or by other authorized official written notice.

INSTRUCTIONS for STANDARD FORM 33

The instructions below correspond to the blocks of the form.

1. Include the DPAS rating if applicable IAW FAR Subpart 11.6 and page information.

2. Insert the award PIIN once you've made award IAW DFARS 204.7003.

3. Insert the solicitation PIIN IAW DFARS 204.7003.

6. Insert the purchase requisition (PR) number from your PR form (i.e., DA 3953, NAVCOMP 2276, AF 9, etc.). This will normally be different from the PIIN.

7. Insert the issuing contracting office information (and its code, if applicable).

8. Leave this blank unless you'll have offers sent somewhere other than block 7.

10. Buyer should place her / his name and telephone number here.

11. Place an "X" in each section included in the solicitation / award and the number of pages in each applicable section.

13. Offeror will insert payment terms as applicable.

14. Offeror will acknowledge any amendments by placing the amendment number(s) and date of acknowledgment.

15. Offeror will include its name, address, and telephone number. If offeror knows its Commercial and Government Entity (CAGE) code and has a remittance address different from 15A, it should insert the CAGE code in 15A and place an X in 15C.

16-18. Offeror will insert the name and title of the authorized signature authority and have that person sign and date the offer before submission to the contracting office.

19. Insert the line item(s) to be accepted. If you are not accepting all line items, ensure you are complying with the conditions for partial acceptance (usually found in section M of the solicitation).

21. Insert the fund cite(s) from which you'll make payment. If the cite(s) will not fit in this block, insert "see schedule, section ?" (usually G) and list your cite(s) in that section.

22. See FAR Part 6.3 for guidance.

23. Insert item 7, 8, 24, or 25, depending on where the contractor should address its invoice to receive proper and timely payment.

24. Leave this blank unless administration functions are done somewhere other than the office shown block 7.

25. Insert the paying address (and code, if applicable).

26-28. Insert the contracting officers printed or typed name and have her / him sign and date. An award is not valid until the contracting officer completes these blocks.

Blocks not explained above are self-explanatory.

SOLICITATION/CONTRACT/ORDER FOR COMMERCIAL ITEMS
OFFEROR TO COMPLETE BLOCKS 12, 17, 23, 24, & 30

			1. REQUISITION NUMBER	PAGE 1 OF

2. CONTRACT NO.	3. AWARD/EFFECTIVE DATE	4. ORDER NUMBER	5. SOLICITATION NUMBER	6. SOLICITATION ISSU DATE

7. FOR SOLICITATION INFORMATION CALL: ▶

a. NAME	b. TELEPHONE NUMBER (No collect calls)	8. OFFER DUE DATE/ LOCAL TIME

9. ISSUED BY	CODE	

10. THIS ACQUISITION IS ☐ UNRESTRICTED OR ☐ SET ASIDE: ____ % F

☐ SMALL BUSINESS

☐ HUBZONE SMALL BUSINESS

☐ SERVICE-DISABLED VETERAN-OWNED SMALL BUSINESS

☐ WOMEN-OWNED SMALL BUSINESS (WOSB) ELIGIBLE UNDER THE WOMEN-OWNED SMALL BUSINESS PROGRAM   NAICS:

☐ EDWOSB

☐ 8 (A)

SIZE STANDARD:

11. DELIVERY FOR FOB DESTINA-TION UNLESS BLOCK IS MARKED ☐ SEE SCHEDULE	12. DISCOUNT TERMS	☐ 13a. THIS CONTRACT IS A RATED ORDER UNDER DPAS (15 CFR 700)	13b. RATING
			14. METHOD OF SOLICITATION ☐ RFQ ☐ IFB ☐ RFP

15. DELIVER TO	CODE	16. ADMINISTERED BY	CODE

17a. CONTRACTOR/ OFFEROR	CODE	FACILITY CODE	18a. PAYMENT WILL BE MADE BY	CODE

TELEPHONE NO.

☐ 17b. CHECK IF REMITTANCE IS DIFFERENT AND PUT SUCH ADDRESS IN OFFER

18b. SUBMIT INVOICES TO ADDRESS SHOWN IN BLOCK 18a UNLESS BLOCK BELOW IS CHECKED ☐ SEE ADDENDUM

19. ITEM NO.	20. SCHEDULE OF SUPPLIES/SERVICES	21. QUANTITY	22. UNIT	23. UNIT PRICE	24. AMOUNT
	(Use Reverse and/or Attach Additional Sheets as Necessary)				

25. ACCOUNTING AND APPROPRIATION DATA	26. TOTAL AWARD AMOUNT (For Govt. Use Only)

☐ 27a. SOLICITATION INCORPORATES BY REFERENCE FAR 52.212-1, 52.212-4. FAR 52.212-3 AND 52.212-5 ARE ATTACHED. ADDENDA   ☐ ARE ☐ ARE NOT ATTACHED

☐ 27b. CONTRACT/PURCHASE ORDER INCORPORATES BY REFERENCE FAR 52.212-4. FAR 52.212-5 IS ATTACHED. ADDENDA   ☐ ARE ☐ ARE NOT ATTACHED

☐ 28. CONTRACTOR IS REQUIRED TO SIGN THIS DOCUMENT AND RETURN ____ COPIES TO ISSUING OFFICE. CONTRACTOR AGREES TO FURNISH AND DELIVER ALL ITEMS SET FORTH OR OTHERWISE IDENTIFIED ABOVE AND ON ANY ADDITIONAL SHEETS SUBJECT TO THE TERMS AND CONDITIONS SPECIFIED

☐ 29. AWARD OF CONTRACT: REF. _____ OFFER DATED _____. YOUR OFFER ON SOLICITATION (BLOCK 5), INCLUDING ANY ADDITIONS OR CHANGES WHICH ARE SET FORTH HEREIN, IS ACCEPTED AS TO ITEMS:

30a. SIGNATURE OF OFFEROR/CONTRACTOR	31a. UNITED STATES OF AMERICA (SIGNATURE OF CONTRACTING OFFICER)

30b. NAME AND TITLE OF SIGNER (Type or print)	30c. DATE SIGNED	31b. NAME OF CONTRACTING OFFICER (Type or print)	31c. DATE SIGNED

AUTHORIZED FOR LOCAL REPRODUCTION
PREVIOUS EDITION IS NOT USABLE

STANDARD FORM 1449 (REV. 2/2012)
Prescribed by GSA - FAR (48 CFR) 53.212

19. ITEM NO.	20. SCHEDULE OF SUPPLIES/SERVICES	21. QUANTITY	22. UNIT	23. UNIT PRICE	24. AMOUNT

a. QUANTITY IN COLUMN 21 HAS BEEN

☐ RECEIVED ☐ INSPECTED ☐ ACCEPTED, AND CONFORMS TO THE CONTRACT, EXCEPT AS NOTED: _____

b. SIGNATURE OF AUTHORIZED GOVERNMENT REPRESENTATIVE	32c. DATE	32d. PRINTED NAME AND TITLE OF AUTHORIZED GOVERNMENT REPRESENTATIVE
2e. MAILING ADDRESS OF AUTHORIZED GOVERNMENT REPRESENTATIVE		32f. TELPHONE NUMBER OF AUTHORZED GOVERNMENT REPRESENTATIVE
		32g. E-MAIL OF AUTHORIZED GOVERNMENT REPRESENTATIVE

3. SHIP NUMBER	34. VOUCHER NUMBER	35. AMOUNT VERIFIED CORRECT FOR	36. PAYMENT	37. CHECK NUMBER
☐ PARTIAL ☐ FINAL			☐ COMPLETE ☐ PARTIAL ☐ FINAL	
8. S/R ACCOUNT NO.	39. S/R VOUCHER NUMBER	40. PAID BY		

1a. I CERTIFY THIS ACCOUNT IS CORRECT AND PROPER FOR PAYMENT		42a. RECEIVED BY *(Print)*
1b. SIGNATURE AND TITLE OF CERTIFYING OFFICER	41c. DATE	
		42b. RECEIVED AT *(Location)*
		42c. DATE REC'D *(YY/MM/DD)*	42d. TOTAL CONTAINERS

STANDARD FORM 1449 (REV. 2/2012) **BACK**

LETTER OF AUTHORIZATION			DATE OF REQUEST 8/23/2007
REQUIRING ACTIVITY (e.g. Army Contracting Agency)	**GOVT AGENCY POC** Doe, John	**GOVT AGENCY POC PHONE** 123-456-7890	**GOVT AGENCY POC EMAIL** lskdjsdjf@tst.com
NAME [Last, First, Middle Initial] Jones, Stanley	**SSN / FIN** xxx-xx-1234	**DATE OF BIRTH** 8/1/1980	**PLACE OF BIRTH**
HOME ADDRESS		**CITIZENSHIP** United States	**PASSPORT # / EXPIRATION** 1234567890123 12/31/2010
		DEPLOYMENT PERIOD START Wednesday, August 01, 2007	**DEPLOYMENT PERIOD END** Monday, September 01, 2008
EMAIL sfdjsk@tst.com		**THEATER EMAIL** test.data@us.army.mil	
CLEARANCE LEVEL w/ AGENCY None	**CLEARANCE DATE** (MM/DD/YYYY) Monday, January 01, 0001	**JOB TITLE** Action Officer	**SUPERVISOR / MANAGER** ☑ / **NON-SUPERVISOR / NON MANAGER** ☐
COMPANY (full name) XYZ Company	**COMPANY POC** Smith, Jane	**COMPANY POC TELEPHONE** 123-456-7890	**COMPANY POC EMAIL** skdljk@tst.com
CONTRACT NUMBER/ TASK ORDER XYZ1234/ABC7890	**CONTRACT PERIOD START** 12/12/2006	**CONTRACT PERIOD END** 12/12/2012	**CONTRACT ISSUING AGENCY** (e.g. DARPA)
NEXT OF KIN (NOK) NAME	**NOK RELATIONSHIP**	**NOK TELEPHONE**	**NOK ALTERNATE TELEPHONE**
IN-THEATER CONTACT		**CONTACT'S PHONE** 029938023984288	**CONTACT'S EMAIL** skdflkjsdfl@tst.com

COUNTRIES TO BE VISITED

Belgium

PURPOSE

Test data

FUND CITE w/ BILLING ADDRESS
Fund Cite
Fund Address,
fund City, 55848
United States

GOVERNMENT FURNISHED SERVICES

☐ APO/FPA	☑ Authorized Weapon
☑ Billeting	☑ CAC/ID Card
☑ Commissary	☑ Dependents Authorized
☑ DFACS	☐ DoDI Essential
☑ Excess Baggage	☑ Fuel Authorized
☐ Medical/Dental	☑ Mil Banking
☑ Mil Clothing	☑ Mil Exchange
☐ Mil Issued Equip	☐ Milair
☑ MWR	☑ Transportation

The government organization specified above, in its mission support capacity under the contract, authorizes the individual employee identified herein, to proceed to the location(s) listed for the designated deployment period set forth above. Non-supervisory positions shall be rated GS-12 or equivalent. Supervisory / Managerial positions shall be rated as GS-13 or equivalent. Upon completion of the mission, the employee will return to the point of origin. Travel being performed is necessary and in the public's service. Travel is in accordance with FAR 31.205-36 and the maximum per diem allowable under the appropriate travel regulations (Joint Travel Regulation (for AK, HI and outlying areas of the United States and US possessions), Federal Travel Regulation for CONUS and US Territories, and Dept of State's Standardized Regulations for OCONUS Foreign Areas designated by DOS).

Emergency medical support will be determined by the appropriate supported commander. Contractor authorization aboard military aircraft will be determined by the supported commander. Necessary identification badges will be determined and provided by the supported command.

This Contractor is considered as "Key Personnel, Government Civilian" in connection with "Non-Combatant Evacuation Orders" at the civil service grade indicated above.

Made in the USA
Coppell, TX
03 April 2023

15129740R00066